D1541420

Don't Quit
Before FINISH
You

Don't Quit
Before You FINISH
You

JIMMY DRAPER

Clovercroft Publishing
307 Verde Meadow Drive
Franklin, TN 37067

Copyright 2015 – Jimmy Draper, All Rights Reserved

Published by Clovercroft Publishing - 307 Verde Meadow Dr., Franklin, TN 37067.

Unless otherwise noted, all scriptures are taken from the Holman Christian Standard Bible®, Copyright © 1999, 2000, 2002, 2003, 2009 by Holman Bible Publishers. Used by permission of Holman Bible Publishers. All rights reserved.

ISBN: 978-1-942557-37-1

Library of Congress Control Number: 2015951875

PRINTED IN THE UNITED STATES OF AMERICA

Book Design and Layout: Russell Lake - SeedStudios.com

First Edition

Don't Quit
Before You **FINISH**

Don't Quit Before You Finish

I met Jimmy Draper in 1954 when I entered university, and our paths have intertwined in ministry ever since, both of us having recently "retired" within five miles of each other and having joined the same church—which both of us pastored! I know this man! I happily commend to you his most recent book, "Don't Quit Before You Finish!" As I perused it, three words came to mind, persistently: "rich, right, relevant." Jimmy's worn many hats, and worn them successfully, but, at heart, he is a life-long pastor, and he magnifies the shepherding ministry in this book. On some of his pastoral anecdotes, I heard myself saying, often, "That story is worth the book." Whether you came to the ministry long ago or lately, whether your church is little or large, this read will bless you. I promise! And as a bonus, Dr. Draper will tell you how to obtain your MBWA degree!

– Bill Anderson, retired Pastor
Calvary Baptist Church, Clearwater, FL

"Don't Quit Before You Finish" is a book I hoped Jimmy Draper would write. Since meeting him in 1976, he has been a role model, friend, encourager and wise counselor. This book should be required reading for every young man or woman considering a calling to ministry. It should be read by every minister who is thinking of leaving the ministry. Brother Jimmy gives us decades of wisdom gained in his personal ministry. He's a leaders leader. He's led great churches as well as his denomination. This is wisdom picked from the abundant fruit of his life and ministry. He has exemplified servant leadership

with great passion and vision for decades. Jimmy Draper is the best combination of pastor, preacher, theologian and listener I've ever known. He's never too busy to write a note, take a call, exegete a passage of Scripture, give a word of encouragement, visit a hospital, lead a difficult meeting or encourage a young pastor.

– Michael Catt, Senior Pastor,
Sherwood Baptist Church, Albany, GA

Jimmy Draper lives a transparent godly life and you can see his footprints and feel his heartbeat on every page of this book. His life is a powerful testimony of one who has lived for Jesus and preached the gospel while concurrently being a "real" person. With the turn of each page, you will learn the valuable and lasting lessons that are realized in the pursuit of honoring Christ in and through your "uniqueness" as a human being and child of God.

Every God-called pastor should read the compelling words of this book at least once a year for the rest of his life. His wife should read it at the beginning of their lives as pastor and wife and intermittingly throughout her life. Every seminary student should be taught this book and each pastor should teach the book to the church leaders within the first six months of accepting the "call" to begin a new journey together as pastor and people. When you read how Jimmy and Carol Ann faced each difficulty and challenge in their lives, and how they *abandoned all of self for all of Christ, you will begin to feel the excitement which is possible in serving Christ as an imperfect, "real" person, forgiven and ready to claim your victories in Jesus.*

– Morris Chapman, former President
Executive Committee Southern Baptist Convention

In my earliest years of pastoring, there was placed in my hands a practical, "How To" book written by a noted pastor of days gone by. That book became an invaluable resource, impacting my life and shaping the way I "did" ministry. To this day, I still practice some of the advice mined from the heart of that experienced pastor. Today, Jimmy Draper's newest book "Don't Quit Before You Finish" is just such a book for every pastor. Here, in four sections addressing the major areas of a minister's life, you'll find counsel for your ministry that is at once practical, scripturally sound, and genuinely effective. Finally the man whom most Southern Baptists would say epitomizes the title of "pastor" has drawn deeply from the well of his heart and the worth of his experience. Jimmy Draper understands you! You will return to this book again and again throughout your ministry.

– Tom Elliff, President Emeritus
International Mission Board Southern Baptist Convention

Reading this book has reminded me what a gift Jimmy Draper has been to the Evangelical church. Wisdom overflows from every page. No matter what stage you are at in your ministry, you will benefit from reading this book and applying these biblical truths and life lessons. Don't be one of the unfortunate statistics. Take these words to heart and finish well!

– Kevin Ezell, President
North American Mission Board
Southern Baptist Convention

Jimmy Draper is a living legend, a man that has personified the spirit of, "Don't Quit Before You Finish." Every Pastor and Christian Leader needs to read this book, regardless of your age. Quitting ministry and life itself can happen at any age; but for those who want to finish strong, abounding with faithfulness, and overflowing with joy can discover the secrets to doing so within this book.

– Dr. Ronnie Floyd, President,
Southern Baptist Convention
Senior Pastor, Cross Church, Springdale, AR

This is the best of books for ministry....written by a great pastor and a Pastor of Pastors! Here preachers can find a rich supply of clear principles, practical illustrations, and marvelous insights from the quotes of highly successful servants of God. Each page reveals the facets of the "high calling of God" for a man seeking to be a Shepherd in the twenty-first century. Jimmy Draper has many strengths and one of those is communicating profound truth in a simple manner so that anyone can understand the message and immediately apply that principle in one's life.

– Nick Garland, Senior Pastor
First Baptist Church, Broken Arrow, OK

"Don't Quit Before You Finish" is written by one of my favorite persons and pastors – Jimmy Draper. You will discover in this book a focus on character, calling, and commitment which will prepare you for a lifetime and legacy of faithful service for Christ and His Church.

– Jack Graham, Senior Pastor,
Prestonwood Baptist Church, Plano, TX

Jimmy Draper speaks from a lifetime of faithful, gospel-centered leadership. He has served as model and mentor to me and so many others, I am excited to see some of his wisdom now put into this volume. This book stirred me, challenged me, and affirmed me. You'll be grateful you read it.

– Dr. J.D. Greear, Pastor
The Summit Church, Raleigh-Durham, NC

To know Jimmy Draper is to love him...and respect him. Through the decades he has led people and pastors as well like King David- "with the integrity of his heart and the skillfulness of his hand." Wise is the young preacher who reads these words and wiser still is the one who heeds them. Read it and reap!

– O.S.Hawkins, President/CEO
Guidestone Financial Resources

While reading Jimmy Drapers book, I felt I was panning in a stream of gold nuggets, saying Amen to nearly every paragraph that flowed from the heart of his sixty years of distinguished ministry. This pastor of pastors has penned one of the very best of all the pastoral books I've read...for newcomers to ministry a primer... to veterans a reminder.

– Jim Henry, Pastor Emeritus,
First Baptist Church, Orlando, FL

Jimmy Draper has been a major influence on my life since I was called to be a pastor as a teenager. He is a model of effectiveness and fidelity in ministry. The practical wisdom in this book doesn't come from the pen of an ivory tower philosopher, but from an authentic leader who has sixty years (and counting) of success under his belt. Anyone who is intent on 'finishing strong' will want to read and re-read "Don't Quit Before You Finish."

– Robert Jeffress, Senior Pastor,
First Baptist Church, Dallas, TX

Serving as a Shepherd of the flock of God in our upside-down world demands a reservoir of wisdom and grace. To read this book is to be invited to drink deeply from Jimmy Draper's reservoir filled through decades of pastoral ministry and service. Wise counsel flows from every page from this master shepherd.

– Dr. Anthony L. Jordan, Executive Director-Treasurer,
Baptist General Convention of Oklahoma

Jimmy Draper has done all of Christendom a tremendous service by writing "Don't Quit Before You Finish." This book summarizes a lifetime of priceless wisdom from one of God's most gracious and winsome servants. Brother Jimmy is beloved by the many thousands he has served as pastor and is treasured by his legion of friends who admire and appreciate his wonderful spirit and deep devotion to our Savior. Every pastor, and would be pastor, should read this book. In fact, they should read this book at least once a year!

– Richard Land, President
Southern Evangelical Seminary

It's one thing to theorize and talk about leadership principles, but it's rare to find someone who has demonstrated a lifetime of modeling them for others. "Don't Quit Before You Finish" isn't a collection of vague buzzwords or empty clichés, but proven wisdom from the fruit of a life well lived. I can attest to these principles being lived out in the legacy of Jimmy Draper as I have the privilege to pastor his two sons and grandchildren. In our shifting world, where culture is debating the future of the church, we desperately need more steady examples like this one. I hope, like me, after reading this book you are more inspired to finish your race and leave a legacy as well.

– Jeff Little, Senior Pastor,
Milestone Church, Keller, TX

Jimmy Draper's new book, "DON'T QUIT BEFORE YOU FINISH", should be required reading at every seminary and Bible College in America! In a day and time when even preachers are trying to be "politically correct," it is good to know that Jimmy wants preachers to be "Biblically correct!" These practical guidelines will help any pastor or preacher not only represent their church well, but more importantly represent God well! Thank you Jimmy Draper for encouraging all of us in ministry to DON'T QUIT BEFORE WE FINISH!

– Fred Luter, Senior Pastor
Franklin Ave. Baptist Church, New Orleans, LA

Jimmy Draper is one of the most respected men I know. I watched him from a distance as a young pastor, and now know him personally from his various roles of leadership and influence. I presently pastor the church where Jimmy Draper pastored for 16 years. Our people still love him deeply and tell many stories of his legendary leadership. "Don't Quit Before You Finish" is an incredibly wise and practical manual that should be read by every person in Christian leadership. The principles in his book are not trendy quips, but the authentic practices of the kind of person God will use in leadership. It's a great read – you won't want to put it down – nor should you! Get it. Read it. Pass it on to other leaders. It will help build the kingdom!

– John Meador, Senior Pastor,
First Baptist Church, Euless, TX

There are authors who write about heroes and then there are authors who are heroes. For all who know Jimmy Draper he falls in the latter category. This is not a book – this is a gold mine for everyone involved in ministry. In fact it is a must read for anyone who is a leader in any organization. Jimmy is universally recognized as the greatest statesman in the largest evangelical denomination in America. This book will minimize your mistakes and maximize your effectiveness in the kingdom of God and, if followed, will ensure you finish well in the race of life. I could not give it a higher recommendation.

– James Merritt, Senior Pastor
Crosspointe Church, Duluth, GA

There are many books available today on pastoral ministry by people who have no or limited experience. Please read them with that recognition. However, this book is filled with practical advice from a man who has been there longer and more profoundly involved than almost anyone. Filled with biblical admonition and true life examples of pastoral wisdom, Jimmy Draper's new book is a must have for pastors, especially young ministers. Listen to his advice, his warnings and to his pragmatic instruction.

– Frank Page, President
Executive Committee of Southern Baptist Convention

Had there been access to Jimmy Draper's book, "Don't Quit Before You Finish," the first 15 years of my ministry would have been incalculably easier for me and a foretaste of the Millennium rather than The Great Tribulation for my parishioners! I do not think that I have ever been so grateful for a lifetime of reflection as I am for this volume and I find it impossible to express how profound is the need for this tome. The first section alone, "You Can't Go If You're Not Sent," is worth six times the price of the book. My advice to any young preacher is simple. Read Three books: The Bible (especially Proverbs), Spurgeon's Lectures To My Students, and Jimmy Draper's "Don't Quit Before You Finish." This will keep your head above water, your body at home, and your heart with the Lord. In two words—simply imperative.

– Paige Patterson, President, Southwestern Baptist
Theological Seminary, Fort Worth, TX

In today's world of Christian publication, too much unproven theory is being written. Young leaders writing to other young leaders about concepts and practices that are nowhere near proven. However, Jimmy Draper's new book "Don't Quit Before You Finish" is the exact opposite. Decades of wisdom and experience ooze from every chapter and provide a valuable resource to every pastor and ministry leader. From calling to character to cultural issues, Jimmy Draper provides Biblical, practical guidance gleaned from decades of faithful ministry. I'm so thankful for the way Jimmy Draper has impacted my life and equally thankful for the impact he's going to have on so many others through this book. I highly recommend it!

– Vance Pitman, Senior Pastor,
Hope Church, Las Vegas, NV

This book should be required reading in every pastoral ministries class. The invaluable practical wisdom for relating to people will enhance anyone's spiritual walk. It is a page-turner. Read it and be blessed!

– Jim Richards, Executive Director,
Southern Baptists of Texas Convention

In a multitude of book endorsements we have all read the phrase, "it should be required reading for every deacon, Christian, husband, etc." Let me go a step further regarding Jimmy Draper's book. Every seminary should have in their budget adequate funds to purchase this work and give it to every ministerial student. This book is scholarly without being tedious, practical without being trite, personal without being presumptuous and instructive without being pejorative. Most importantly, I know the author and nothing in this book is hyperbole, exaggeration or self-aggrandizing. No man is more qualified to write this classic work. Thank God he did.

– Bailey Smith, Evangelist, Duluth, GA,
former Pastor
First Southern Baptist Church, Del City, OK

I regret having read Jimmy Draper's book "Don't Quit Before You Finish." That is, in July, 2015. I wish I could have read it in July, 1957, the year I began my pastoral ministry! It would have spared me some heartaches. And more than one foolish mistake. These words of practical wisdom from one of Southern Baptists' most effective pastors and administrators will be invaluable to young pastors. Jimmy Draper's commitment to Christ and integrity in ministry shine forth on every page. Profit from this man of God who isn't quitting before he finishes.

– Jerry Vines, former Pastor
First Baptist Church, Jacksonville, FL.

In ministry and life what matters is not how you start, but how you finish, so every pastor should read this book! It is jam-packed with the practical wisdom of one who has made it successfully for over 60 years. Jimmy Draper has been a spiritual father to thousands in ministry and now he has condensed a lifetime of learning into this volume. Read it and buy a copy for every pastor you know.

– Rick Warren, Senior Pastor
Saddleback Church, Lake Forest, CA

Just memorizing the Table of Contents is certain to change your life! This book is the best of the best. Read it and receive eternal benefits!! We've never needed this more than now!!

– Bobby Welch, 32 years Senior Pastor
First Baptist Church, Daytona Beach, FL.
Global Strategist for Executive Committee of
Southern Baptist Convention

In a day of vanishing authentic Christocentric Leadership, this book "Don't Quit Before You Finish" is a timely gift and a breath of fresh air to the Body of Christ! This book is a clarion call to serve effectively and finish strong. (2 Tim.4:6-8)

It provokes genuine repentance, remembrance, revitalization and refreshment in me! It reminds me of who I am and whose I am and that my life is all about magnifying and glorifying the name of the Lord through radical obedience to His will and His word!! (1 Cor.10:31) I believe that this book is a MUST READ that will challenge and encourage every God called Pastor-Preacher-Prophet, to passionately pursue the Prince of Peace which will ensure the faithful fulfillment of His calling on our lives!! (1 Cor. 9:16)

With blessed transparency, Jimmy Draper shares rare godly wisdom that will equip and encourage us to be a dramatic demonstration and illustration of incarnational truth manifesting the power of God in our person, which is a primary prerequisite for leadership!

Thank you Jimmy Draper, for this relevant and life changing word, I pray that it will usher in a revival of Godliness and Holiness in Leaders, that will be a catalyst to fix fractures, revolutionize relationships and realities as we walk as Kingdom citizens of all ethnicities, with our Redeemer!!! "... for it doth yet appear what we shall be..." 1 John 3:2

– K. Marshall Williams Sr., Senior Pastor,
Nazarene Baptist Church, Philadelphia, PA and
President, National African American Fellowship, SBC

Jimmy Draper has never quit before he finished. He is certainly a great example of a man who is faithful in service to our Lord and is finishing strong in his journey of faith. His book is rich with insight on making the most of God's calling and being faithful in ministry, and it includes a multitude of quotes to hold onto. I look forward to sharing this book with many people in the future.

– Bryant Wright, Senior Pastor,
Johnson Ferry Baptist Church, Marietta, GA

Jimmy Draper is a man of wisdom and integrity, committed to the calling God placed upon his life so many years ago. His new book, "Don't Quit Before You Finish," provides practical advice for those of us who share the same calling. As pastors and preachers, we are called to be change agents and that comes at a price. The frontlines of Christianity continue to place us in vulnerable and often lonely positions. Thankfully, we have dedicated servants like Jimmy Draper to undertake the task of writing directly to fellow pastors with words of encouragement and direction. He has manned the front for over sixty years and continues to stay in the battle!

– Ed Young, Senior Pastor,
Second Baptist Church, Houston, TX

Don't Quit Before You Finish

DEDICATION

To Carol Ann, who has walked by my side for over 60 years. Her example of faith, devotion and compassion has inspired me every day since I met her in 1955. She has exemplified the fruit of the spirit, the anointing of God and the patience of Job with the frantic pace the Lord has had for us throughout this journey. She has never complained with all the challenges we have faced and has cheered me on in every assignment the Lord has had for us. It has truly been "our ministry" for all these years. It has been her support and encouragement that has brought these pages to reality. In every way she is a Proverbs 31 woman. Her children "rise up and call her blessed. Her husband also praises her: Many women are capable, but you surpass them all!" (vs. 28-29) I thank God for her today and praise her with all the fervency of my heart as I write these words. She is God's perfect complement for me and has shown me more of the grace of God and the integrity of her heart than I could ever deserve. Thank you, sweetheart, for who you are and for Whose you are. You have made the journey a delight and endless blessings over these years.

Don't Quit Before You Finish

TABLE OF CONTENTS

Foreword.. i

Introduction v

SECTION ONE:

You Can't Go If You're Not Sent

Make Certain of Your Call.. 2

Don't Neglect Your Personal Relationship
    With the Lord.. 18

Don't Fail Your Wife and Family................................. 22

God Really Loves the Church – So Should You! 26

Always Be an Encourager 33

Never Make a Decision When You Are
    Discouraged or Depressed 41

Doubt Never Means "Yes".. 43

Don't Let Anger Be a Pattern for Your Behavior.......... 47

Let Your Preaching/Teaching Flow From the Bible 49

There's No Excuse for Being Unprepared to
    Preach/Teach.. 53

Don't Flirt With Temptation 56

Be Careful In Your Contact With the Opposite Sex.... 59

Be an Example of Integrity.. 63

Don't Fall Into the Money Trap 66

You Are a Steward of Your Position and Influence...... 69

Don't Be Surprised By Opposition 73

You Can't Please Everyone!.. 81

Be Quick to Forgive Mistakes 84

SECTION TWO:

Christian Leadership is Being a Servant

Servant Leadership is the Key........................ 90

Be Open and Honest 102

Always Respond When People Contact You 104

We Need Each Other 106

Build Strong Relationships........................... 110

Cherish and Protect Friendships..................... 114

Keep Confidences...................................... 116

Lead By Example 118

When You're Wrong Admit It.......................... 120

Be a Grateful Person.................................. 122

Don't Be Disloyal 127

Don't Take Criticism Personally And Don't
    Believe All the Praise You Get Either............... 129

Learn To Listen – Or You'll Never Learn! 133

You Work With Others–They Don't Work for You... 140

Don't Be Threatened If People Love
    Their Former Minister 142

Face Problems Head-On and
    Deal With Them Quickly 144

Responsibility Without Accountability
    Is Dangerous 149

Pay Attention! Remember Names!............... 151

SECTION THREE:
Dealing with Change

Don't Be Afraid To Change 156

Demonstrate Courage. Don't Avoid Risk! 164

Let's End Racial Prejudice Now! 168

Always Share Your Faith... 179

Keep a Good Sense of Humor. Learn
      to Laugh At Yourself...................................... 183

Manage Your Time Well.. 186

Give Clear Directions and Expectations 192

Have a Positive Attitude.. 195

Meet People on Their Turf 199

Learn to Delegate.. 201

Write Notes of Concern, Consolation
      and Appreciation 204

Every Church Needs Regular Financial Audits 208

Be an Advocate for Your Co-Workers........................ 210

Dealing With the Search Committee 212

So You Have a New Position 216

How To Leave a Church 218

Guard Your Tongue...And Pen...And Email!.............. 221

Always Accept Resignations 223

Be Generous With Departing Co-Workers................ 225

Learn From Your Failures.. 227

Continually Stretch Yourself. Raise The Bar! 230

Prepare ror the Unexpected 234

Evaluate Your Strategy 236

SECTION FOUR:
This is God's Ministry!

Be Ambitious for God's Kingdom 242

Demonstrate Humility 244

Communicate the Vision 254

Be Redemptive 257

Perception Is the Cruelest Form of Reality 263

Everyone is of Great Value 265

Never Compromise Your Convictions 266

Don't Panic! 270

Keep Your Eyes On the Goal 272

Don't Quit! 274

EPILOGUE: Embrace Obscurity 280

FOOTNOTES 293

BIBLIOGRAPHY 301

Don't Quit
Before You **FINISH**

JIMMY DRAPER

FOREWORD

If you were to look up the words servant leader in the dictionary you would probably find the face of Jimmy Draper. He is known across the Southern Baptist Convention as the Pastor to Pastors. For over 50 years now he has served local churches and has ministered to Pastors. Only Heaven knows how many phone calls, emails and especially how many personal cards and letters he has written and sent to be an encouragement to those who lead our churches. To say that he has exemplified the model of Servant Leader is the understatement of the new millennium.

I consider Jimmy Draper my father in the ministry; even though he was not the man that led me to the Lord. Soon after my conversion I had the opportunity of visiting the First Baptist Church of Euless Texas where I saw and heard him for the first time. Not long after our initial meeting he took a very special interest in investing in my life. God used him to challenge me to attempt to influence the generation coming behind me. Through that challenge the ministry of Timothy + Barnabas was born. Now as a result of his influence thousands and thousands of Pastors have been impacted across our Southern Baptist Convention along with dozens and dozens of other nations of the world. I am one of the thousands of Pastors that have been impacted by this man's ministry.

Now at 80 years of age God is greatly blessing the local church in that Jimmy Draper has written this book <u>Don't Quit Before You Finish</u>. I could not put the manuscript down when I began to read it. I was encouraged to familiarize myself with this book in order to write this forward. But instead of familiarizing myself by reading a few chapters I read every single word. Whether he was challenging me on God's call on my life, building strong relationships, making my family a priority, guarding my attitude, being faithful in my preaching, being aware of temptation, being a man of integrity, how to deal with money, the list goes on and on of the most practical everyday occurrences in the life of a Pastor. This book is literally an absolute must read for every Pastor, every staff member and every leader in the local church.

My life has been so impacted by reading it that I am asking special permission to use so much of it in preparing lessons in teaching Pastors in the United States and abroad.

Jimmy Draper not only served as Pastor for 35 years but he also was used of God to lead the Sunday School Board, which is now Lifeway Resources. Having served there 16 years he continued his ministry of touching Pastors by bring in Pastors' Round Tables, starting ministries and encouraging ministries that help hurting Pastors.

One only needs to know a little bit about Jimmy Draper to know that he has a big heart and lots of his life and moments committed to helping those who lead our local churches.

I wish I could purchase this volume and place it in the hands of every Pastor and staff member in the Southern Baptist Convention. I hope as you read it you will reminded of the importance of the call God has given us. The privilege that is ours and as a result the accountably that will be required comes with such responsibility. All of those subjects and so many more are dealt with in this book.

Thank you, Jimmy Draper, for this invaluable ministry to each of our lives.

Johnny Hunt
Former President Southern Baptist Convention
Pastor, First Baptist Church Woodstock, Georgia

Don't Quit Before You Finish

INTRODUCTION

It's been 63 years since I entered college as a freshman. I was a 17-year-old young man chomping at the bit to dive in and experience all campus life had to offer. The years I spent on campus are still among some of the best of my life—a true Camelot experience in every sense of the word. I have often said I would still be there if I could!

For an enthusiastic young fellow like me, college life opened up a whole new world of experiences and opportunities—friends to make, lessons to learn, adventures to have. The campus was literally buzzing with energy from hundreds of young men and women like myself, excited about our newfound freedoms and the endless possibilities that lie ahead. Our professors were challenging and personally engaged in our lives outside the classrooms. Even our football team was full of promise, enjoying nationally ranked status at the time. Those days still hold a magical charm for me.

There was lots of good-natured hazing from the upperclassmen now and then, but I let it be known that I could certainly hold my own when it came time to repay the favor with a spirited prank. Some of my fondest memories center around the jokes we played on one another during those years and the friendships formed. Among those closest to me were a group of 25 young men who had surrendered to the ministry as the calling for their life's work.

Though we all had different backgrounds, different hopes and dreams for our futures, and different skill sets, we all had one thing in common:

WE WANTED TO CHANGE THE WORLD FOR CHRIST!

Now, some 63-plus years later, many of those friendships are still going strong, but only four of us have remained in the ministry full-time for our entire lives. That's not to say that many of those men haven't and aren't still impacting the Kingdom—they have and they are!—though primarily in laymen and/or leadership positions within their churches. Sadly, though, many of the young men from those early days haven't weathered these many years with their faith and personal witness still intact.

But how does this happen? What causes a group of young men fully committed, fully convinced of their calling, and fully capable of serving in the ministry, to become little more than a statistical demographic of 20-something collegiates? What did these men overlook, overstep, or disregard in terms of living out the Lord's calling on their lives? Was it one cataclysmic event or a series of missteps? A clash in theology or interpretation of doctrine? Decidedly intentional or quietly subtle?

If young men, once on fire for the Lord and passionate about His Kingdom, can so easily falter, burn out, or worse, what about the rest of us? What do we ignore or discount or misconstrue when it comes to fulfilling the Lord's calling on our lives? How can we hope to live and serve in such a way that God is honored? His good name protected? Our integrity above reproach? How can we earnestly seek His anointing for our lives?

The answer is simple and straightforward; the implementation, however, is anything but simple.

Life comes at each of us lightning fast. Friends and family may disappoint us; some will even betray. Critics, competitors, and coworkers may attack and undermine our intentions, even condemn our best efforts. We make one decision based on this belief or expectation only to change our mind and our perspective and react in a completely different manner when the circumstances change. We fast learn that doing what is right in the eyes of the Lord affects not just how others see us, but how we view ourselves, too. Add to this the ever-present opportunities for all of us to compromise on matters of faith, morality, and ethics, and the fallen nature of man become painfully clear even among the most committed.

The Evangelical world has been rocked for decades with men and women who have failed morally and ethically and, consequently, brought shame and dishonor to the Kingdom. Lapses in judgment, shifts in perspective, and far-flung rationalizations daily affect ministry leaders and their followers. The fall-out ultimately brings disgrace to Christ's honorable name. And so remains the question:

HOW CAN WE REMAIN TRUE IN THIS SINFUL WORLD?

In the last 50 years alone, there have been far too many contradictory examples of leaders who have answered the call—some stumbling before global audiences while others remain godly examples, steadfast in their convictions and commitments to Christ and others.

Why do some who begin their ministries with such intention and intensity fall prey to the flattering words of men, the temptation of women, and the lies of entitlement? What is it about them that leads to a shift in their perspective that causes them to lose sight of the very things that led them to the ministry? How do they allow the short-term to totally short-circuit the broader, grander picture without any regard to the moral, ethical, or even criminal implications of what they do? And finally, how can they not consider that whatever remains of their legacy will forever be tainted by their misdeeds?

What separates the disgraced man from the one who completes the race; the one who, in the end, justly receives honor and respect for his sacrificial life of faithful service? Why can one man remain strong in his commitment to the calling of the Lord while another falls so tragically? Why is one's career marked by doubt, disloyalty, and poor choices while another leaves behind a legacy of steadfast effectiveness, loyalty, and respect? How can two men, equally gifted and potentially effective, end up so differently?

It is no news that current trends in culture have become overtly hostile towards Christians. As a result, it is no wonder so many leaders of the faith have succumbed to this growing, outside pressure. Temptations to compromise our basic convictions are more prevalent, persistent, and subtle than ever before. It is not uncommon anymore for believers who are serious about their faith to face ridicule and openly aggressive hostility if they seek to live by the principles of God's word.

The recent ruling by the Supreme Court, which redefined marriage, has taken our society as a whole one step closer towards open hostility to the Christian faith. And yet, as believers, we cannot allow changing culture to force us to accept what the Bible condemns. For modern day Christ-followers, every day brings with it a new challenge to our ministry.

Beyond the agenda of the homosexual community, national apathy towards abortion has reached an all-time high. A staggering 57 million preborn children have been murdered since 1973 and the total grows more substantial by the day. For children that are allowed to make it to term, the odds of them being born to a single mother with no father figure present throughout their life is higher than ever before. This abysmal breakdown of the nuclear family unit will increasingly threaten the welfare of our country for generations to come.

All of these significant and seismic shifts in culture and more have combined to make it increasingly difficult for each of us to stay strong in our faith, true to our character, and unwavering in our ministry. And yet, the charge remains: We are called to live and minister in such a way that God is pleased and others see consistency, honesty, kindness, and godly character in us throughout all our lives.

That's what this book is all about.

The principles and guidelines contained herein will not only insure that we serve effectively in the beginning, but also that we finish strong. God wants our lives to ring true to our calling to follow Him and lead others throughout the duration of our lives, not just in the early days when inexperience and enthusiasm fuel our ministry. We are each called to complete the race He sets before us, not quitting or compromising until the end when we long to hear the words of our Lord, "Well done, good and faithful servant."

This book is intended to help you become a better leader, not a better manager. John Kotter distinguishes between the two in his book, "Leading Change," this way: "Management is a set of processes that can keep a complicated system of people and technology running smoothly...Leadership is a set of processes that creates organizations in the first place or adapts them to significantly changing circumstances. Leadership defines what the future should look like, aligns people with that vision, and inspires them to make it happen despite the obstacles."[1] See the difference? It's remarkable. As believers, we are all called to be leaders, not managers, of the life-changing, soul-saving news about Christ's life, death, and resurrection, and what it means for us in the 21st-century.

Again, that's what this book is all about. The message of Christ has not changed for over 2,000 years, but the methods of communicating this truth to others must continually be evaluated and adapted. Christ is culturally relevant no matter our societal norms. It remains our commission to convey this to a world of unbelievers. The principles of Christianity have never been complicated or difficult to understand. They have always been practical and grounded in biblical truth and revelation. And they have always called for consistency, integrity, and a life beyond reproach.

Put these principles into your life's actions and God's blessings will attend your ministry. One by one these guidelines will reveal you to be a person of godliness, integrity, fairness, firmness, faithfulness, and compassion—all the hallmarks of a committed Christ-follower and leader.

Take to heart this old admonition: "Your life is God's gift to you. What you make of it is your gift to God," and your days will be fruitful.

Stay strong in your ministry and don't quit before you finish!

–Jimmy Draper
Fall 2015

Don't Quit Before You Finish

Don't Quit
Before You FINISH

1

You Can't Go if You're Not Sent!

Make Certain of Your Call

The ministry is a terrible vocation…but a wonderful calling. I remember the first time I heard that old saying it gave me pause and made me think just a little deeper about my chosen profession. Fortunately, the Bible is crystal clear that God's ministry involves a calling from God. Without this divine call, the job would simply be too much to carry.

In "Point and Purpose in Preaching," Elijah P. Brown makes the case for receiving a true calling to the ministry when he says, "The man who would open the Bible for people to live and die by ought to know beyond all chance of doubt that God has sent him to do it. If he doubts this, the probabilities are that he will do more harm than good in the pulpit." [2] Brown's words are convicting to say the least.

There is insistence by some today that God does not have an individual call for our lives. In his book, "Pastor to Pastor," Erwin Lutzer points out, "it is not uncommon for some believers to insist that there is no need for a specific call from God to ministry." [3] This falsehood has been promoted in large part by Garry Friesen in his book, "Decision Making and the Will of God." In it, Friesen states, "that God has a sovereign will (His overall plan) and a moral will (His guidelines for life and belief), but no individual plan for every believer." [4] Sadly, many have bought Friesen's conclusion.

From a biblical and historical standpoint, this is unequivocally false. The idea that God does not have an individual plan for each one of us totally contradicts the testimony of Scripture and betrays the significant precedent of history. Each of us should firmly believe that we are committed to live the life God has called us to live.

In the Yale Lectures of nearly a century ago, John Jowett charged his audience with these words: "Now I hold with profound conviction that before a man selects the Christian ministry as his vocation he must have the assurance that the selection has been imperatively constrained by the eternal God. The call of the Eternal must ring through the rooms of his soul. 'Necessity is laid' upon him. His choice is not a preference among alternatives. Ultimately he has no alternative: all other possibilities become dumb: there is only one clear call sounding forth as the imperative summons of the eternal God…If we lose the sense of wonder of our commission, we shall become like common traders in a common market, babbling about common wares." [5]

That's a visually strong comparison—a marketplace vendor hawking his goods and services versus a lukewarm preacher, questioning his divine appointment. And yet, Jowett's words ring true to those certain of their calling. With the Lord's conviction of a calling, the power of a preacher's words could never be interpreted as 'babbling.'

Lutzer concurred with Jowett and even cited Charles Spurgeon as a wise counselor to prospective ministers: "Spurgeon discouraged men from entering the ministry. He told them plainly that if they could take another vocation they should. He wanted only those who felt strongly that they had no other alternative. They were called of God." [6]

For me, the journey into the ministry began when I was 12 years old. I was at church camp at Piney Woods Baptist Encampment near Groveton, Texas and I struggled through a fitful night full of convictions, conflicts, and questions. Though I felt certain of the call to ministry, I thought at the time I had to know exactly what God wanted me to do. Was I to be a pastor, an evangelist, a missionary, a music minister, an educational minister, or even a professor? I was overwhelmed at the options and relieved to realize by morning's light that I did not have to know the precise task God has called me to do.

For the next two years, the call of God on my life intensified to the point that, by the age of 14, I knew beyond a shadow of a doubt that God was calling me to preach the Gospel and to serve Him in a uniquely special way. My moment of clarity came during a youth-led revival in Jacksonville, Texas. I was standing on the back row of the choir praying for a close friend I had witnessed to. And as clearly as any voice I have ever heard, God said to me, "How can you expect your friend to be saved when you are not willing to do what I want you to do?"

That was the time and place I was unmistakably called by God, to be set apart for His use in a special way. In every moment since, I can go back to that unforgettable moment when God called me to the ministry. It was a defining moment for me. It was a moment clearly ordained by God.

In one of the best-selling books of all time, "The Purpose Driven Life," Pastor Rick Warren explains the reason for our very existence: "The purpose of your life is far greater than your own personal fulfillment, your peace of mind, or even your happiness. It's far greater than your family, your career, or even your wildest dreams and ambitions. If you want to know why you were placed on this planet, you must begin with God. You were born by His purpose and for His purpose." [7]

It's so simple and straightforward and yet, we so often cloud the issue with our doubts, rationalizations and exceptions. Consider the following admonitions from the Bible concerning His people accepting and embracing His direction for them:

> When God would build a nation of His unique people, He said to Abraham, "Go out from your land, your relatives, and your father's house to the land that I will show you...so Abram went, as the Lord had told him..." –Genesis 12:1, 4

When He would lead His people out of Egypt He presented His plan to Moses:

> "Then the angel of the Lord appeared to Moses in a flame of fire within a bush. As Moses looked, he saw that the bush was on fire but was not consumed. So Moses thought: I must go over and look at this remarkable sight. Why isn't the bush burning up? When the Lord saw that he had gone

over to look, God called out to him from the bush, 'Moses, Moses!'

'Here I am,' he answered….'I am sending you to Pharaoh so that you may lead My people, the Israelites, out of Egypt.'" –Exodus 3:2-4, 10

When God would lead His people in the Promised Land, there was Joshua: "…the Lord spoke to Joshua son of Nun, who had served Moses: 'Moses My servant is dead. Now you and all the people prepare to cross over the Jordan to the land I am giving the Israelite. I have given you every place where the sole of your foot treads, just as I promised Moses…No one will be able to stand against you as long as you live. I will be with you, just as I was with Moses. I will not leave you or forsake you.'" –Joshua 1:1-3, 5

When He would set aside a prophet who would anoint the first King of Israel, God came to Samuel. Four times in 1 Samuel 3, it says, "The Lord called."

When He would set Isaiah in the King's court as His special spokesman, Isaiah encountered his call: "Then I heard the voice of the Lord saying: 'Who should I send? Who will go for Us?' I said: 'Here I am. Send me'" –Isaiah 6:8

Ezekiel's testimony is the same: "In the thirtieth year, in the fourth month, on the fifth day of the month…the word of the Lord came directly to Ezekiel the priest…And the Lord's hand was on him there." –Ezekiel 1:1, 3

The Old Testament is filled with examples of the prophets using phrases like "The word of the Lord came," or "The Lord said," or "This is the Lord's declaration." These men clearly served under the compulsion of the call of God on their lives.

These verses illustrate the absolute willingness of so many men to drop everything for the opportunity to follow the Lord:

Matthew 4 tells us, "As He was walking along the Sea of Galilee, He saw two brothers, Simon, who was called Peter, and his brother Andrew...'Follow Me,' He told them, 'and I will make you fish for people!' Immediately they left their nets and followed Him. Going on from there, He saw two other brothers, James the son of Zebedee, and his brother John...and He called them. Immediately they left the boat and their father and followed Him." –Matthew 4:18, 19-22

In Matthew 9, we learn that Jesus called even tax collectors such as Matthew – "As Jesus went on from there, He saw a man named Matthew sitting at the tax office and He said to him, 'Follow Me!' So he (Matthew) got up and followed Him." –Matthew 9:9

Matthew 10 says, "Summoning His 12 disciples... Jesus sent out these 12 after giving them instructions:..." –Matthew 10: 1, 5

Luke 10 describes the call and instructions given to 70 other special messengers: "After this, the Lord appointed 70 others, and He sent them ahead of Him in pairs to every town and place where He Himself was about to go." – Luke 10:1

When God would open the Gospel to the Gentiles, He sent Philip as it is told in the Book of Acts: "An angel of the Lord spoke to Philip: 'Get up and go south to the road that goes down from Jerusalem to Gaza." –Acts 8:26

The very next chapter of Acts recounts the dramatic conversion of Saul of Tarsus—a calling of legendary means. Saul's calling was nothing short of miraculous by any measure: "As he traveled and was nearing Damascus, a light from heaven suddenly flashed around him. Falling to the ground, he heard a voice saying to him, 'Saul, Saul, why are you persecuting Me? 'Who are You, Lord?' he said. 'I am Jesus, the One you are persecuting,' He replied. 'But get up and go into the city and you will be told what you must do.'" –Acts 9:3-6

When God first shared that the goal of the local church was to send missionaries to the ends of the earth, He chose the church at Antioch and called His men: "As they were ministering to the Lord and fasting, the Holy Spirit said, 'Set apart for Me Barnabas and Saul for the work I have called them to.'" –Acts 13:2

Paul is diligent to mention his specific call or describe the ministry to which God has called him in every epistle he wrote.

To the Ephesian elders, he wrote, "Be on guard for yourselves and for all the flock that the Holy Spirit has appointed you to as overseers, to shepherd the church of God, which He purchased with His own blood." –Acts 20:28

And finally, he points out that the pastoral office is a direct gift from God: "And He personally gave some to be apostles, some prophets, some evangelists, some pastors and teachers, for the training of the saints in the work of ministry, to build up the body of Christ." –Ephesians 4:11-12

The lack of certainty of a divine call to the ministry is one of the main reasons why almost half of seminary students leave the ministry within five years after leaving seminary. The sacrificial life of ministry is simply too demanding and too stressful to endure without the certainty of a calling directly from the Lord. You simply cannot maintain your commitment to service without this assurance.

Esteemed Southwestern Baptist Theological Seminary professor Dr. Jeff D. Ray put it like this, "If a man goes into the ministry because he wants to, while in it he will conduct himself as he wants to and go out of it when he wants to, but if he realizes that he is put there by the sovereign call of God, he will try to please God while in it, and he will stay in it till he receives a divine summons to give it up." [8]

When speaking of what is required of young men called to the Lord's service, Charles Spurgeon said, "Or ever a man stands forth as God's ambassador, he must wait for the call from above." [9]

On another occasion, Spurgeon states the charge clearly: "I preach because I cannot do otherwise; I cannot refrain myself; a fire burns within my bones which will consume me if I hold my peace." [10]

The testimonies of many great and godly preachers unanimously confirm the idea that one must be called from God to sustain a life of service, but history is also full of extraordinary men who concur:

> "Every minister, before he undertakes to preach the Gospel of the Lord Jesus Christ, ought to be able to say 'the Spirit of the Lord is upon me because He hath anointed me to preach the Gospel.'" [11] –John Wesley (1703-1791)

> "I was quite willing to preach the Gospel. Nay, I found that I was unwilling to do anything else. I had no longer any desire to practice law. Everything in that direction was shut up, and had no longer any attractions for me at all. I had no disposition to make money. I had no hungering and thirsting after worldly pleasures and amusements in any direction. My whole mind was taken up with Jesus and His salvation; and the world seemed to

me of very little consequence. Nothing, it seemed to me, could be put in competition with the worth of souls; and no labor, I thought, could be so sweet, and no employment so exalted, as that of holding up Christ to a dying world." [12]

–Charles Finney 19th century
lawyer-turned evangelist

"God alone knows how deep a concern centering the ministry and preaching was to me. I have prayed a thousand times, till the sweat has dropped from my face like rain, that God…would not let me enter the Church before he called me and thrust me into his work." [13]

–George Whitfield, 18th century evangelist

Of Whitefield's resistance to accept his calling, his biographer concluded, "Notwithstanding this dread of the ministry, Whitefield knew he was called of God to its labours and that before long he must enter upon it. Yet as he viewed its responsibilities and remembered his own weakness, he felt he could undertake it only if he received such an assurance from heaven, that he could consider it a Divine commission." [14] Strong but effective words concerning a man who ultimately led thousands to the Lord.

Christian leaders of the 20th- and 21st-century confirm a call to preach the Gospel must come from Christ alone:

"I made a solemn covenant with God that while I lived I would never have any other business or profession or calling than to preach the Gospel—to give myself wholly to that, 'sink or swim, live or die, survive or perish,' to turn back to any other never, never, never forever." [15]

–B. H. Carroll, founder
Southwestern Baptist Theological Seminary

"At youth camp in 1965, with the call of God thundering in my heart, I knelt at a prayer garden in Latham Springs Baptist Encampment, and surrendered my life to the ministry." [16]

–Jack Graham, Senior Pastor
Prestonwood Baptist Church

"The call, the incessant pounding of the Holy Spirit in my heart, led me to get on my knees one Saturday night, by my bed, and I prayed something like this: 'Father, if you are calling me to be a minister, I will give you my best. Don't let me do or say anything to bring shame on your name, and I will follow you the best I know, wherever you lead me in my life.'" [17]

–Jim Henry, former Pastor
First Baptist Orlando, FL

"My call to the ministry was so clear and certain I have never doubted that call." [18]

–Junior Hill, Evangelist, Hartselle, AL

And again from Junior –

"Lovingly, gently, but persistently He took away from me that which I liked so that He could eventually give me that which I would love. He steered me from the path I had devised to the steps He had directed…The Lord was calling me to preach and I knew it—and furthermore I also knew that would never again have peace in my heart until I had wholeheartedly submitted to that call." [19]

And finally, from the man who has brought God's word to so many amid the chaos of Las Vegas:

"I was raised in church but it wasn't until I was a freshman in college that I finally began a real relationship with Jesus Christ. For the first time in my life, I began to be consumed with a passion to know Him intimately. Through the relationship, God began to speak into my life about a call to preach. I could not escape the constant drawing I sensed from the Holy Spirit. When God speaks, it is always clear. I was reading Jeremiah 1:1-10 and as soon as I read it I knew for sure that God had called me to preach the gospel. I knew it was so certain that if I did anything else I would be miserable. I surrendered my life to this call. That has been 20 years ago now, and let me just say that the call of God is absolutely essential to this work. I cannot stop what I didn't start. If I had chosen to preach, I can and would have chosen to do something else a thousand times. But the reality is He chose me. The joy of the ministry is knowing I am obeying His call out of the overflow of my relationship to Him." [20]

–Vance Pitman, founding Pastor
New Hope Baptist Church, Las Vegas, NV

Perhaps the greatest biblical illustration of the necessity of a divine calling is found in the life of Jeremiah. Despite his protests, the Lord spoke convincingly and compassionately to Jeremiah in this passage,

"The word of the Lord came to me:
'I chose you before I formed you in the womb;
I set you apart before you were born.
I appointed you a prophet to the nations.'
But I protested, 'Oh no, Lord, God! Look, I don't know how to speak since I am only a youth.'
Then the Lord said to me:
'Do not say, "I am only a youth," for you will go to everyone I send you to and speak whatever I tell you.

Do not be afraid of anyone,
For I will be with you to deliver you.
This is the Lord's declaration.'
Then the Lord reached out His hand, touched my
mouth, and told me:
"I have now filled your mouth with My words."
                                        –Jeremiah 1:4-9

A little bit about Jeremiah helps explains much of his hesitancy to represent the Lord. He was originally from Anathoth, which had been established by Abiathar, David's great high priest. Sometime around 640 B.C., King Josiah came to the throne as an eight-year-old boy and was quite possibly a childhood friend of Jeremiah.

Both boys assumed tremendous responsibility from a young age: Josiah was charged with turning the nation of Israel back to God; Jeremiah was called to be a prophet. When Josiah was approximately 26 years old, the Book of the Law was found in the Temple and the high priest, Hilkiah, passed the book on to Shaphan, the king's scribe. Upon hearing its words, Josiah tore at his clothes, repented of his sins, and humbled himself before God. The young king's humility marked the beginning of the most far-reaching religious reforms in the history of Israel to that point. Sadly, for all the reform that initially occurred, genuine and lasting change did not remain in Israel.

Meanwhile, Jeremiah was growing in knowledge and influence. As a member of the upper class, he was constantly surrounded by scholars, priests, and prophets, and considered the aristocratic leaders of his time as peers. Jeremiah's knowledge extended well beyond the academics of the day; he was well versed in many of the deeper things of God. He was well informed and well disciplined and enjoyed a God-given ability to understand and interpret the meaning of the events of his day.

Not surprisingly, the call upon his life was completely transformational. He came to realize that God had chosen him for a great task even before he was born. He also realized that he could never escape the reality of the call that drove him to faithfully proclaim what God had told him to say. He was clearly a man set apart by God and gradually began to accept that nothing he faced could separate him from the destiny that the call of God on his life dictated.

Although Jeremiah was weak and untrained, he was prepared to hear the voice of God and came to accept the calling God had placed upon him. Jeremiah could be considered 'Exhibit A' regarding the often-quoted phrase:

God doesn't call the equipped;
He equips the called.

In their book, "Liberating Ministry from the Success Syndrome," Kent and Barbara Hughes echo this principle.

They say, "The practical point for us here is that when God calls one to the ministry, he gives the requisite gifts to fulfill that ministry...He very often calls those who obviously would not be able to fulfill their calling apart from his gifts." [21]

I cannot overstate the importance of listening when it comes to dealing with matters of God. The most gifted man in the world will not hear the call of God if he is not listening. Similarly, the weakest and least-gifted man will hear the call if he is listening. Time and time again, the Bible gives us reassuring examples that the Lord calls and equips ordinary men—men like you and me—to serve Him and His people. Virtually every shortcoming we see within ourselves can be used for the Lord's glory if we are obedient to His calling. Don't allow your doubts to discourage you from the Lord's calling and don't consider a life in ministry without being certain of your call.

The Apostle Paul understood the importance of his divine calling when he said, "For I was appointed a herald, an apostle...and a teacher of the Gentiles in faith and truth," (1 Timothy 2:7) and went on to confirm, "How can they preach unless they are sent?" (Romans 10:15). Men do not choose to preach; they are chosen to preach.

God's call to ministry is distinct from every other vocation a man may have. Though other professions allow men to separate their professional lives from their private ones, there is no room in the ministry for living a double life. It is 'all in' in every aspect of a man's life and those who attempt to separate their ministry from their personal life are doomed to fail eventually. For those in the ministry, they must live out their sermons daily and set the example of holiness and devotion before their followers and the outside world.

Wherever you find yourself today—considering the ministry, preparing to preach, even years into service—I have two powerful words for you going forward: confirm and magnify.

Confirm your call.
Magnify your ministry.

Ours is a call from the sovereign grace of our Lord. We are saved by grace and we serve by grace. God never uses us because of us, but always in spite of us because He loves us and chooses to use us! Relish your call and celebrate it often in your heart, soul, and mind!

1 Don't Neglect Your Personal Relationship with the Lord

It is imperative for pastors, preachers, ministers— anyone leading others on their spiritual journey—to be always growing and maturing in the Lord. Every day your relationship with the Lord should be stronger than the day before. This must remain a priority throughout your time in the ministry because it is all too easy to allow the urgent and the anxious to squeeze out the time it takes to build and maintain an ever-deepening relationship with Christ.

The resistance to set aside this time will be present throughout your time of service. Push past the resistance, plan for it, and overcome it. If you neglect to give your relationship with the Lord the attention it needs, you will soon find yourself busy with the work of God, not the will of God.

Though constant availability through the Internet and cell phones have compounded this battle of time vs. will, it is certainly not a new challenge for those who serve. This quote from "The Pastor: His Qualifications and Duties" dated back to 1879 proves this has been a long-fought battle: "The men who deal with spiritual things must themselves be spiritual... Spiritual force comes from within, from the hidden life of God in the soul. It depends, not on mere outward activities, but on the divine energies acting through the human faculties, God working through the man, the Holy Ghost permeating, quickening all the powers of the preacher, and speaking his voice to the souls of the people. The soul's secret power with God thus gives public power with men, and the mightiest influences of the pulpit often flow from a mere utterance of man: there is in it a power more than human." [22]

You cannot possibly be prepared to face the demands, expectations, opposition and negativism inherent in ministry if you do not have a vital relationship with the Lord. Stay close to Him! You cannot expect to lead someone where you have not been, through experiences you have not had, and through challenges you have not faced. Dependence on the Lord will be the lifeline through which you survive and thrive.

Some days, the only thing that will keep you going is the knowledge in your heart that the Lord has, in fact, called you to do what you do. That is why your personal walk with the Lord must remain steadfast and unwavering regardless of the circumstances. Your ongoing dependence on and conversation with Christ will keep you in constant awareness of your call. Through this, He will continually make clear His calling and intentions for your life. Find comfort in knowing that your calling is unique to you, a sacred trust the Sovereign One has placed upon and within you. You show your most genuine gratitude for this privilege through disciplined time alone with Him.

The best and most fruitful of this time with God is through prayer—speaking to and listening to God. Your most beneficial prayer times will not be spent asking for things, even spiritual things, but will be listening for Him to speak His message to you. The words you receive are for you— where you are at the time, the issues you face at the time, and those you hold influence over at the time. Because all these variables are constantly changing, a constant dialogue with God is your best preparation for covering every word you speak and every action you take with prayer.

The carry-over effect of your praying life as a leader can have a far, far-reaching impact on your followers. The ripple effect of a praying pastor can transform, heal, and ignite a congregation like nothing else. Pastor Michael Catt has witnessed, first-hand, this blessed phenomenon: "Everything good in my life and in the life of the church I pastor, I attribute to praying people. Every blessing has come from a prayer environment. Every time I've seen Satan win the day, I know we've let our prayer guard down. And every time we've moved forward as a church family, it has been on our knees." [23] That's a strong, declarative statement. He didn't say 'most times' or 'usually' regarding his congregation's prayers; he said 'every time' for the good and the bad. Every time.

You can rest assured that you will never have a praying church unless you set the example as the pastor of being deeply committed to praying in your own life. It is also only through a regular, personal relationship with God can you reveal the reality of who you are in Christ. You can fake it with some, pretending to be something other than you really are for only so long. When your relationship with God is going full throttle, all pretenses are destroyed. You can't help but reveal your true, God-given character. It is, after all, the essence of who you are, who Christ made you to be, and is of utterly no surprise to Him. The radiance of all God made you to be can only be seen, can only bless others, and can only bring glory to His Kingom, if yours is an effective relationship.

My final admonition regarding the importance of your walk with the Lord comes from J. Kent Edwards' book, "Deep Preaching." In it he says, "Deep sermons cannot be preached by shallow people. Profound sermons only come from people who enjoy a profound relationship with God. Like it or not, the condition of our personal relationship with God will control our public ministry for God." [24]

Powerfully true words.

1   Don't Fail Your Wife and Family

Without doubt, your first line of ministry is your family. If you fail there, you have failed in your calling. Strong words, I know, but complete truth. Put your wife and children on your calendar for dates and events and honor them as consistently as you would any other appointment—even more so! It is the wise pastor who realizes the intense need to minister to his family, taking the time and making the effort to show them they are of utmost importance to him. The recipe for this end goal is simple: consistent time, strong communication, and intentional effort.

In "Winning in the Land of Giants," William Mitchell says, "Time, communication, daily disciplines, and a giving, caring atmosphere are the hallmarks of a good home life. When we lose sight of these basics and let them slide, families begin to unravel, and eventually, the very fabric of our social structure starts to come apart." [25]

Your relationship with your wife should always reflect the importance you place on her place in your joint ministry. Publicly praise her and make certain she receives the just credit for her significant contribution, both at home and church. Your partner for life is your best line of defense and will be your greatest support in ministry. You should both work to let your members see your relationship with each other as one of faith and faithfulness.

You must know this mutually supportive partnership doesn't come without significant work from both parties. Every marriage needs polishing to keep it shining with the glow of new love and pastors are no exception. Set weekly dates with your spouse and don't allow interruptions to preempt them. There will always be committee meetings, calls to make, and members to counsel; however, your original commitment to your wife should almost always take precedents. By reassuring your wife that she is an integral part of your shared ministry and second only to the Lord in your eyes, you will cultivate an atmosphere of support and strengthen your marriage and ministry at the same time.

Unexpected cards, calls, gifts, and getaways are terrific ways to shore up a union that began strong but that can sometimes take second place to growing responsibilities within your church. The impact of a joyful marriage between a pastor and his wife is a witness that sets the tone for marriage throughout an entire church—challenging husbands to love and cherish and wives to honor and respect. The rewards are passed on for generations as children learn and grow in such environments.

I've often heard it said that the best thing a dad can do for his children is to love his wife and I wholeheartedly agree. If this is what your children learn, it is what they consider to be the standard. Set the example in such a way that it brings honor and glory to Christ's plan for marriage.

I realized early on that pastoring a growing congregation and involvement in association-related activities meant I was gone many evenings. As a result, I tried to be home as much as possible when my kids came home from school. This usually meant throwing the football or baseball with my boys or setting aside time just to hear about my daughter's day. My wife made early dinners to help make it possible for us all to be together at least once a day. It was a valuable lesson I took to heart from my earliest days: Don't minister to everyone else and lose your family in the meantime.

I Timothy 3:4 reminds us that a leader is "one who manages his own household competently, having his children under control with all dignity." And Titus 1:6 describes a church leader as, "one who is blameless, the husband of one wife, having faithful children not accused of wildness or rebellion." It takes time and intention to develop this kind of relationship with your family.

I saw a tragic example when this commitment to family was absent. Bob Pierce was the founder of World Vision and led that organization remarkably effective for many years. His organizational leadership and ministry's growth ultimately came at the expense of his wife and children. In her book, "Days of Glory, Seasons of Night," Pierce's daughter, Marilee Pierce Dunker speaks of her father's choice of ministry over family. In emotional detail, Dunker says her father's neglect of his family was tremendously substantial, often being gone as long as 10 months at a time. These lengthy absences eventually cost Pierce his marriage, the tragic suicide of one of his daughters, and a lonely death. Take heed from Pierce's missteps: if a leader is careless and becomes so engrossed in his own personal calling, he runs the risk of losing his family at the expense of his ministry.

This lesson of putting family first dates back to Moses' challenge to the people of Israel when he said, "Only be on your guard and diligently watch yourselves, so that you don't forget the things your eyes have seen and so that they don't slip from your mind as long as you live. Teach them to your children and grandchildren" (Deuteronomy 4:9).

Charles Swindoll has preached 'the indoctrination of children' to a life of faith has always been the primary responsibility of the parents, and not something to be delegated to outsiders such as 'institutions or the combined efforts of a groups of professionals.' And that all such teaching was to be 'deliberate' in nature. [26]

I urge you, no beg you, to make much of your responsibility before God to teach and train your children. They will learn from watching you whether it is good or bad.

They need to learn from your example and your lips as you teach them the basics of the Christian faith. Being present for your family is a ministry non-negotiable.

James Merritt put it succinctly: "If you don't lead your children, someone else will lead them for you. If you are not there for your children, someone else will be there for them—someone you may not like. When that happens, the greatest problem is not that you won't be around, but that you will no longer be missed." [27]

The bottom line: your marriage and family are your highest priority, second to your relationship with the Lord. Don't take care of everyone else's family and lose your own in the process. Spend time with them, shower them with love, encouragement, and appreciation—never let them doubt you're their biggest supporter! The church and the world need to see the example of a solid Christian family filled with genuine love and gratitude for each other and the Lord.

1

God Really Loves the Church… And So Should You!

The Word of God is perfectly clear about the church. In the very first book of the New Testament, Jesus says, "…I will build My church, and the forces of Hades will not overpower it." (Matthew 16:18) He didn't say the church would be without challenges, persecution, and internal struggles. Nor did He claim the church would remain untarnished. But He did say, ultimately, it would not be overcome by Satan.

In "Serious Times, Making Your Life Matter in an Urgent Day," James Emery White presents his perspective regarding the powerful presence of the church: "Jesus made this staggering claim because the church would be his ongoing incarnation on planet earth. The church is his body, his presence, his life—the means for his ongoing ministry to the world, not simply as the universal body of believers around the world but as concrete communities of faith gathered together in the name of Christ as mission outposts to the world. And you cannot fulfill God's plan for your life, much less change the world, apart from taking your place in its mission and ministry, community and cause." [28]

Jesus made it clear that the church was a fluid body of believers, never to be constrained by actual temples, sanctuaries, or other such structures. In fact, Jesus commanded the followers of His day to go and share well beyond the church's perimeters. In Matthew 28: 18-20, Christ shares His expectations for his followers: "... 'All authority has been given to Me in heaven and on earth. Go, therefore, and make disciples of all nations, baptizing them in the name of the Father and of the Son and of the Holy Spirit, teaching them to observe everything I have commanded you. And remember, I am with you always, to the end of the age'" (Matthew 28:18-20).

Paul, visibly humbled by the trust of Christ's calling upon his life, wrote this passionate plea to the church in Ephesus, "Therefore I, the prisoner for the Lord, urge you to walk worthy of the calling you have received, with all humility and gentleness, with patience, accepting one another in love, diligently keeping the unity of the Spirit with the peach that binds us" (Ephesians 4:1-3). Paul knew the saving grace of Christ and remained unwavering in his conviction to urge others to fulfill their calling, stay true to the divine strategy at work in their lives, and to follow Christ as Head of the church.

Paul's admonition does an excellent job of recognizing the true nature and function of the church. He knew, and fervently preached to others, that the church was not a human institution and therefore, was not expected to devise its own strategy nor set its own goals. It was never intended to be an independent organization, but rather a body of believers called into a special relationship with God.

Paul uses several word pictures to describe the relationship between the church body and Christ. Throughout Scripture, he characterizes the church as a body under the control of its head Jesus Christ (Ephesians 4:12-16), as a temple of worship (1 Peter 2:4-5 and 1 Corinthians 3:16, 6:19-20), and as an army commanded by its King, Jesus (2 Timothy 2:3-4).

When the church is faithful to its calling, it becomes a healing agency in the face of our societal ills. It is not an afterthought with God; it is the intentional manifestation

He designed to be a source of community for Christians. God planned the church before the world was made, not after. His first concern is, and always has been, not what the church does, but what the church is. The directive is clear: being must always precede doing, for what we do will follow what we are.

It is important to remember that the first task of the church is not the welfare of men. The priority of the church is to praise and glorify God. The challenge of the church is to lead an unknowing and unbelieving world to the saving knowledge of Jesus. In doing so, a church honors the Lord to the highest realms of heaven.

The fullness of Christ has always been best seen in His body of believers. Ephesians 2:19-22 explains this well: "So then you are no longer foreigners and strangers, but fellow citizens with the saints, and members of God's household, built on the foundation of the apostles and prophets, with Christ Jesus Himself as the cornerstone. The whole building being put together by Him, grows into a holy sanctuary in the Lord. You also are being built together for God's dwelling in the Spirit."

It's amazing how the invisible Spirit of God can bring together people from all walks of life, with little else in common save a belief in the incredible presence of Jesus Christ in their lives. That, in a nutshell, is what makes the church so incredibly profound, so mysterious to many.

The church is, inherently, the dwelling place of God and this dwelling is ultimately in the hearts and souls of God's people. Since the beginning, the church has had and continues to have one responsibility: to make visible the invisible Christ, to declare in word, and demonstrate in character, the redemptive work of God in Christ.

Longtime Bible scholar Warren Wiersbe is exceedingly clear about the critical role the church plays when he says, "The only hope for the world is the church, and the only hope for the church is to return to worship. God must transform His people and His church before he can work through us to meet the crushing needs of a world lost in sin." [29]

It is far too easy for the church to talk about displaying the character of God without backing these claims with Christ-honoring actions. Speaking without follow-through brings no honor to Jesus. The actions of the church best represent the love of the Lord when they act in humility, patience, love, unity, and peace. These traits are the true hallmarks of Jesus.

Alone, the church cannot save the world, however, the Lord of the church most certainly can! The church focused on exalting itself cannot also exalt the Lord—it will always be one or the other. Love for the Lord and one another must always be the benchmark against which a body of believers tests itself. In the Book of John, Jesus tells his disciples the true litmus test of their devotion to him when He says, "'I give you a new command: Love one another. Just as I have loved you, you must also love one another. By this all people will know that you are My disciples, if you have love for one another.'" (John 13:34-35).

Love is never manifested by rivalry, greed, ostentatious displays, indifference, or prejudice. Love is concerned with maintaining unity, not creating it. The church can never create unity; only maintain it. It is the church's command to introduce a new dynamic to a lost world—the dynamic of the life of Jesus Christ. It is our job as members of His church to make known to all we meet that the risen Lord Jesus Christ is available to men, women, and children everywhere to implant within them His own life and transform them into loving, concerned, confident people, fully equipped to cope with whatever problems life may set before them. This is clearly the calling of the church.

A sense of community and belonging should be the goal of every church professing to follow and bring others to Christ. Church leaders and their members are to be blind to the differences that bring so much division in society. Ethnicity, race, socioeconomic standing, and other classifications that cause divisions among people are to be non-issues within the church.

"We were created with the need for belonging, and if the church is to be relevant, the first need we should meet is this need for community. I would even venture to go a step further and say it is impossible for us to be the church God had in mind if we do not offer authentic, loving, warm environments where people can belong in healthy community," says David Putnam in his book, "Breaking the Discipleship Code." [30] Putnam draws a definitive line in the sand when it comes to the church offering authentic love.

Every ministering staff member should covenant with God to never do anything to hurt the church. It should be crystal clear to all staff, laymen, and members that the Lord Jesus Christ is the head of the church and the earthly leader of the church is the pastor. If you serve in a role other than pastor, make it a priority to offer your full support and loyalty. If you are a pastor, you must realize that you are a servant leader and your role is to help each of your fellow partners in ministry to be successful. Together, the staff must speak with one voice and have genuine love and respect for one another to create an environment of trust and growth.

If you ever get to the place where you cannot be a supportive team member, then it is time for you to serve elsewhere. But please, leave your position before you bring any injury to the church and determine, in advance, that you will leave without bitterness or malice towards anyone within the church. You will honor God if you do so and, in turn, God will honor your efforts.

As Paul concluded in the third chapter of Ephesians, God can outpace us at every turn, in every manner. Hear his closing prayer, "'Now to Him who is able to do above and beyond all that we ask or think according to the power that works in us—to Him be the glory in the church and in Christ

Jesus to all generations, forever and ever. Amen.'" (Ephesians 3:20-21). As hard as we may try, we truly can't grasp the magnitude of God. He is able to do infinitely more than we could ever imagine in a thousand lifetimes! We can't out-ask, out-think, out-dream, out-imagine our God. He is able to do exceedingly and abundantly above all we ask or think.

This is true in our individual lives and the life of the church as well. Whatever we aspire to regarding our church—the growth, the revival, and presence of servant leadership—whatever! God can still go beyond that! The Great Commission was given to the church for a reason: It is His expectation that through the sharing of His word, the church will bring glory and honor to Him. He has placed the church in the center of His strategy when it comes to worldwide redemption. Regardless of our official titles, as Christ-followers, we are all to love the church, lead the church, and touch the world through the church.

Always Be an Encourager

My dad always reminded me to "Be kind to everybody, because everybody is having a hard time." His words have stayed with me throughout my life and have never been more important than when I was pastoring a church. Showing kindness towards and sensitivity to those whom you serve is vital. It's truly amazing how small efforts can make tremendous strides towards strengthening relationships.

Writing notes of appreciation, making calls of concern, and showing thoughtfulness will do wonders towards cultivating supportive friendships among those you serve.

Every single person needs encouragement at some time or another; most of us more than we'd care to admit. This was the strongest admonition my dad gave to me as I began my career as a pastor. The challenge of Dad's words are similar to the challenge Paul spoke to the Ephesian leaders, telling them to, "...be kind and compassionate to one another, forgiving one another, just as God also forgave you in Christ" (Ephesians 4:32).

You can be firm and convicting in dealing with others without sacrificing kindness along the way. In fact, as a rule, encouragement should follow criticism whenever possible. The well-known Christian lay preacher Howard E. Butt, Jr. addressed this in his book, "The Velvet Covered Brick." Butt used this contradictory title to reflect his personal leadership style, showing the need for a strong and unwavering sense of conviction (the brick) softened by kindness and tact (the velvet) when dealing with others.

As a pastor, you will find that nice guys really can finish first...and finish well. The bulldozer effect, running down everything in your path, is never the best way to deal with issues and conflicts among your staff or congregation. There is always a case to be made for being kind in your presentation, regardless of the actions of others.

Former President Theodore Roosevelt became known for his folksy approach to resolving conflict. His "speak softly, but carry a big stick" slogan was more of a handy phrase to sell newspapers and really less reflective of his governing style. For Roosevelt, his life was decidedly more about speaking softly than brandishing a big stick. His kindness with friends and strangers alike was well documented.

Following his presidency, Roosevelt took a monumental trip to explore the outlands of Brazil. During the expedition, a majority of his companions lost their lives to malaria and other environmental threats. When offered the only bed on the boat, Roosevelt repeatedly declined and chose instead to sleep on the wooden deck alongside his fellow explorers. His simple sacrifice of comfort for camaraderie showed he was "in it" with them and not to be treated as special in any way.

Another example of exceptional leadership was General Robert E. Lee. Lee was uncharacteristically loved by soldiers on both the North and South sides because he chose to endure the same hardships as his men rather than claiming the perks of his position. In a show of solidarity, Lee oftentimes refused to eat when his men were hungry, refused the warmth and shelter of officer headquarters when his men were cold and miserable, and he chose not to wear the fine clothing of an officer while his troops were so ill clad. Much of the reason Lee is considered a great American hero is because of his own attitude of kindness.

Stories have been passed down for generations about the extreme kindness of George W. Truett, former pastor of First Baptist Church, Dallas during the days of The Great Depression. Because the church has always been in the shadow of downtown Dallas, the homeless of the city would often congregate near the sanctuary front steps. When the temperatures fell throughout the winter, Truett was known to give a man the coat off his back. This happened more times than people could keep track of and, as a result, the deacons were seriously conflicted when it came time to hand over the deed to the parsonage for fear he would somehow justify giving away his home! Dr. Truett was a legendary, generous giver. It was the heart of his greatness.

Dr. Truett is also great example that it doesn't take some tremendous, magnanimous act to make a positive change in someone's life. Many of us have dreams of one day doing something greatly heroic, forever benefiting mankind. In reality, what the world needs most are simple acts of daily kindness—simple, unexpected courtesies that oftentimes require little effort on our part, but mean the world to others. Phone calls of concern, the quiet ministry of your presence in times of sorrow, and shared laughter in times of rejoicing all go a long way to deepen our relationships.

Through the years, I've come to appreciate how very much it means to my ministry when I show genuine concern and interest in my staff, their families, and the families that make up my congregation. People want to know that they matter to you—that you know their name, their kids' names, and something about what is going on in their lives. It's a lot to ask of a pastor to make such significant of an investment in the lives of so many, but it ultimately serves to further Christ's Kingdom and set the example for them to model to others.

I vividly recall learning that one of our editors at LifeWay had just lost his daughter in a car accident following her graduation from high school. I immediately called him from the hotel parking lot in another city where I was involved in a meeting. We cried together, hundreds of miles apart, and I was privileged to minister to him in his time of such extreme sorrow. I can't tell you what I said that night, and I don't think that's what's important—what is important is reaching out and being available to others in times of crisis.

Sometimes the crises in others' lives aren't so obvious or extreme, but are present nonetheless. How we handle things in these cases can be tricky and frustrating and seemingly fruitless. Other times, they can be our most effective ministry. This was the case for me one day when I was serving as president of LifeWay and my assistant announced that a very angry customer from another state was on the phone demanding to speak to me. He had talked to other people in the curriculum area but hadn't received the response he wanted, and was now intent on talking to the president.

I fount out he was in charge of the curriculum for his church and his order had not been fulfilled to his satisfaction.

When he had called to correct the order, his frustration soon reached fever pitch over the responses he received from our staff. The longer he told his story, the angrier he became. When I got on the phone he continued to complain angrily. At one point he finally asked, "Well, are you even a Christian?"

Quite honestly, I was offended and angry at his pointed question and my response said as much, "Of course, I'm a Christian!" I bellowed.

My anger did little more than add to his as he managed to say, "Well, I can tell this conversation is going nowhere," before he slammed down the phone.

In the silence of my office, I could hear the unmistakable voice of God say to me, "You didn't handle that very well." I knew in my heart I hadn't and the Lord confirmed it. My only choice was to call the man back and correct it.

When he answered, I told him I wanted to apologize, "Gene, you asked me a very legitimate question, and I did not respond properly to you." Then I related my conversion experience to him, apologized again, and assured him that the problem was ours and we would take care of it appropriately and immediately.

When I finished speaking, I heard him weeping on the other end of the line. Through his tears he managed to say, "You know, these last two months have been the hardest months of my life," and from there, he began to pour out his heart over what he had been experiencing.

And then I realized…he wasn't mad at us; he was mad at lot of other things and people in his life—we were just the ones who caught the fall-out of his frustrations.

His life was literally falling apart around him and our disappointing responses had been 'the straw that broke the camel's back' in terms of what he could (or couldn't) handle. A simple mistake on our part had pushed him too far and we were on the receiving end of his built-up anger for all that was happening in his life. In the end, we resolved his order to his satisfaction. I was able to speak a bit of encouragement and perspective into his life, and I was reminded how important it is for kindness to characterize all of our relationships with others.

Years before this experience, I had the opportunity to see first-hand the power words of affirmation can have even on the most unlikely of characters. The church I was serving had purchased an answering system that allowed people to receive a message from me and leave a message for me or our staff. I would tape a message and then, with a bank of phones at our offices, volunteers would call our church members and ask if that had time for a message from the pastor. When they agreed, my recording would come on with my message and at the end I would ask, "Is there anything I can do for you today?" The system would record their responses and they would then be forwarded to me. The success of the system and our offers of help and service were such a success, it was reported in the Wall Street Journal.

During one of the recording sessions for these messages around Christmastime, I was in Dallas at a recording studio. The technician who helped me was a big, husky, bearded young man from Minnesota—not exactly a cuddly kind of fellow! I read my script and ended the recording by reminding our members "I love you very much" and told them I was grateful for them.

When the recording was a wrap, I looked over at my technician friend who had begun to cry. When I asked what was wrong, he said, "Do you realize how many people never have someone say to them, 'I love you'?" It was an honest question from a hurting heart. From that tiny recording booth on a cold and wintry day I was reminded how crucial it is to encourage everyone whose path you cross throughout the day and how important the slightest expression of love can be someone.

Regardless of your staff or membership size, make the effort to show your concern for them and their families. Send messages of concern, write notes of encouragement. Every individual has milestones in their lives worth noting. Each birthday brings with it a cause for recognition; each death provides time for encouragement to those grieving, and each birth is a joyful cause for celebration of a new life. Anniversaries, special achievements, crisis moments, and special occasions are all opportunities for reaching out through a phone call, a handwritten note, or an email.

My encouragement for you is to remain intentional in your efforts to reach out to your people and to look for ways to serve them. In doing so, your small acts of kindness and words of support will become the best testimony of the Lord's love living in and through you.

Never Make a Decision When You Are Discouraged or Depressed

My dad always told me that I should be content where I was before God could lead me somewhere else. It's a pretty simple principle, but carries much truth with it. I understand that sometimes circumstances override this principle, but more times than not, it is true that when we are discouraged or depressed, we will usually make the wrong decision. When we feel these emotions, it is almost always a sure-fire indication that we are not in close relation with the Lord.

All too often, as pastors, we allow the busyness of our ministry to cause us to neglect our relationship with the Lord. The result is that we end up doing the work of the Lord, but not taking time to be with the Lord. Keep in mind throughout your career, you can never make up by doing, what you lack in being.

Make it a priority to take the time to refresh yourself, recharge your battery, and get rest. Sometimes the most spiritual thing you can do—for yourself and others—is to take a nap! Exercise is another wonderful way of fueling your mind, body, and soul, and can give you significant time alone with God. Retreats and sabbaticals are also tremendously beneficial ways to restore your heart and spirit. By taking breaks throughout the days, weeks, and months of a year, you are best able to get and keep your heart on fire and challenged by what is before you. A heart full of excitement for the ministry God has given you is the best tonic there is for a discouraged and depressed heart.

Frequently, one of the most common sources for discouragement among pastors is in numbers—their numbers—those reflecting membership, baptisms, offerings, mission support, and so on. But all these numbers amount to nothing in terms of measuring God's approval for you and your ministry. It doesn't matter if they're dismally low or exceedingly high, it's all relative to your point of comparison, and most importantly, irrelevant to God. What we consider to be 'high' numbers can sometimes give us a false sense of security and success in ministry. Sadly, they can also obscure the reality of a life without a strong and growing relationship with God. The most important requirement God makes for all of us is to be faithful with what He has given us to do and, none of it can be measured in the statistics of baptisms, budgets, and buildings. No measurable ministry number means more to the Lord than our one, individual relationship to Him.

We show our love and respect to Him best when we are faithful and true to His calling for our lives and the assignments he places in our paths. This obedience can only be measured in our heart and through our daily walk with Christ. Don't allow the ebb and flow of attendance numbers and professions of faith to cloud your commitment with discouragement and despair. When our focus remains upon Him, there is little room for anything but gratitude to fill our hearts.

Doubt Never Means "Yes"

I am a firm believer that God never leads us through doubt. If you do not have peace about a decision, your answer should be 'no' or 'wait.' If God is God, and He most assuredly is, then He has a plan for your life and is more than powerful enough to give each of us clear and unequivocal guidance in the decisions we face. James reminded us of a call to action whenever we face doubt and indecision: "Now if any of you lacks wisdom, he should ask God, who gives to all generously and without criticizing, and it will be given to him." (James 1:5).

God may lead you through a compelling call to serve elsewhere or release you from your current ministry or present unexpected opportunities, but He will never lead you through doubt. The check in your spirit, the hesitancy of your heart, the second-guesses are intended to give you pause and prevent you from making a wrong, ill-informed decision. You don't have to know the will of God; you do have to be committed to doing it. Many of us want to know the will of God so we can consider it. God wants us to know His will so we can do it! Commit yourself right now to do whatever God desires and designs for you to do and He will make His will clear to you. The key in dealing with God's will is to commit to doing it before you know it.

I learned the value of this lesson even before my twentieth birthday. Carol Ann and I were engaged to be married by my junior year at Baylor and her senior year in high school. We had fallen deeply and completely in love despite the 200 miles that separated us at the time. Wisely, her parents thought it important for us to spend several days together before we made the whole 'for better and for worse' commitment to one another so they brought her to Waco for a long weekend.

One day we were visiting the home of close friends in the city, listening to music, and thoroughly enjoying the company of each other. As we listened and talked, we soon began to realize that we had become so enamored with one another that we could hardly fathom what we each would do if something were to happen to the other. The more we talked, the more convicted we became and soon found ourselves kneeling before God, making a covenant commitment to Him and promising obedience to His calling for the rest of our lives.

I don't remember the words exactly, but I do know we said something like this: "Dear God, if something happens to

Jimmy or Carol Ann, we'll each keep serving you and loving you for all of our life. Our answer is 'yes' to whatever you want us to do. Reveal your will to us and we will obey it immediately. We will not argue with you, debate your direction, or attempt to negotiate with you. We will fully submit to you whatever it may involve. For now, and the rest of our lives, our answer is 'yes!'

That has been the consistent practice of our lives some 60+ years later. Looking back at a full and varied life of ministry, we both honestly believe that we have never made a decision to move or accept a position that God did not ordain for us to have. We have been blessed by many offers and opportunities, but have remained steadfast in our commitment to go only where God is leading, no matter how attractive the offers have been. By making this decision before we knew what His will would be each time, we've always known He was present in whatever decision we made. This has been key to a life free of regret and poor life decisions.

If you will get on your knees before God and pledge to obey Him whatever He desires for you to do, He will guide you and use you throughout every phase of your life. When you do this, you are surrendering to be faithful and obedient, no matter what the plan. God's assignment for you may change, but it won't matter when you have already submitted to His will.

Charles Stanley explains it this way: "When we obey God, we will experience His blessing; when we don't, we will miss out on that blessing. The more familiar we become with God's Word, the more we will begin to understand obedience. God's laws are not designed to deprive us of pleasure or prosperity; rather, they are intended to protect us from hurting ourselves and others, and to guide us toward the fulfillment in life that He wants us to enjoy." [31]

I have always said and believed that God called me to preach. To this day, I still believe that is my basic assignment, but through the years, God has taken me on many assignments that did not require me just to preach. For every church assignment I've ever had, I have always served as pastor. Eventually, God called me to be the president of the Sunday School Board of the Southern Baptist Convention. This group is now known as LifeWay Christian Resources of the Southern Baptist Convention. When I was in this role, I preached regularly, but it was not my primary assignment.

By serving in such a varied position after pastoring several churches, I was able to see that I wasn't called just to preach. First and foremost, I had been called into a relationship with Christ and, in this relationship, He could assign me to whatever task pleased and best served Him. My job was to be obedient to whatever that task was and wherever it took me.

Settle this in your heart here and now. Give your 'yes' to God and allow Him to use you as He best sees fit. By committing to the desires of His heart, you will be given clarity of calling and clear direction concerning life's biggest decisions. If doubt does creep into your consciousness, take it as a sign—a sign that, for now, your answer is either 'no' or 'wait' and rest in the comfort that the Lord will remove all doubt.

Don't Let Anger Be a Pattern for Your Behavior

1

At the very least, those of us in the ministry should be known for treating others with kindness and courtesy—especially those that disagree with us. You can disagree, be firm in your position, even be offended, but responding in anger is a dangerous response. You should always take a step back and take a few deep breaths before you respond to others out of anger and rage.

The pulpit is not a suitable place for anger, either. I've seen plenty of preachers in my time, who seem to be full of anger as they share their sermons with their congregation. I understand the fierceness of righteous indignation, and know it has its place in ministry, but I can't help but consider every opportunity I have to preach a joyous opportunity to share the grace of God. There's no room for anger when you're presenting the critical truths of God's Word.

I learned the power of choosing kindness over anger while still in college. When one of my favorite professors, Dr. Kyle Yates, came to Baylor University to teach, I was a junior. I became his first grader and came to know him intensely well through the two years of our interactions. To that point in my life and since, I have never had the privilege of knowing a kinder, more gracious Christian man than Dr. Yates. Intrigued, one day I asked him how he came to be this way and he told me it all began while he was teaching at Southern Baptist Seminary.

While there, in an 8 a.m. class he had a student who slept through most of his classes. After several weeks of putting up with this young man's total lack of attention, Dr. Yates reached a breaking point. He woke the young man, criticized him in front of the whole class, and pointedly told him not to come back if he couldn't stay awake in class in the future.

After the class was over, another student confided to Dr. Yates, "I wish you hadn't done that," he explained. "That guy's wife is dying of cancer in the hospital and he spends his nights there with her. He comes directly to class each morning and then goes to work for eight hours before heading back to the hospital."

"After that," Dr. Yates said, "I determined then to never act out of anger or hostility again."

Since we never fully know the challenges and circumstances of others' lives, it is always more Christ-honoring if we speak and act out of kindness, keeping our anger in check.

Let Your Preaching and Teaching Flow From the Bible

1

Preaching, teaching, expositions, exhorting—are they really different? And, if so, what's the difference? The short answer is yes; they are different though they're frequently used interchangeably when it comes to words from a preacher. In their simplest description, preaching means to proclaim or teach; teaching means to educate and instruct; exposition means interpreting or explaining; and exhorting means urging or encouraging. Generally similar words, each with a distinct meaning.

Regardless how you characterize your message, it is of utmost importance that Scripture is the basis for all your words. Don't work to discover topics that you consider worthy of presentation and then try to find Scripture to substantiate your message. Start with Scripture and let your message grow from there.

A regular discipline of careful and prayerful Bible study will always help you to keep your message grounded and relevant to contemporary needs. You can't guarantee God will bless your creative interpretation of societal norms, but you can be confident His Word will always be blessed. When you saturate your preaching and teaching with Scripture in a text-driven manner, you can be sure your words will be spirit-filled.

The challenge of allowing our own perspectives, prejudices, and feelings to color and affect our sermons has been around as long as there have been pastors. Look carefully at these quotes, some from more than 100 years ago to better gain a glimpse into the perspective of preachers past:

From 1912 –

"What is a sermon? A sermon is an oral address to a general audience with a view to unfolding, elaborating, and enforcing Scriptural truth. What is exposition? In preaching, exposition is the detailed interpretation, logical amplification, and practical application of a passage of Scripture." [32]

From 1890 –

"It is manifest that to take a text gives a certain air of sacredness to the discourse. But more than this is true. The primary idea is that the discourse is a development of the text, an explanation, illustration, application of its teachings. Our business is to teach God's Word." [33]

And, from 1924 –

"A preacher may have popular gifts and qualities, but he is a weaponless warrior in the thick of the battle, unless armed with the sword of the Spirit."[34]

Today, more than ever, we are confronted with the questions, 'How do we know truth?' and 'What is the basis of our knowledge?' To these questions, I say there are only three possible answers:

1) We identify what we consider to be truth and use as the basis of our knowledge through relativism, reason, or rationalism;

2) We identify what we consider to be truth and use as the basis of our knowledge our religion or the church – which translates to believing whatever stance the church takes as the final authority on a subject;

3) We identify what we consider to be truth and use as the basis of our knowledge revelation from God.

As believers, we should be comfortable believing and defending our beliefs based upon whatever the Word of God says, trusting that it is the final authority and basis for all truth. Everything we need by which to live is found in Scripture. When you saturate your sermons with Biblical principles set in the proper context, you help others to see the application for their lives and know your words will not be wasted. God will bless you when you speak His Word.

I like Fred Lybrand's description of preaching and teaching from his book, "Preaching on Your Feet": "Preaching is actually about winning the listener to think, feel, and act in accordance with the biblical truth at hand. Some times that object is faith in Christ, but at other times it may be letting go of a root of bitterness that has held one captive for decades. The Word of God is the Word from God, and the object, simply put, is to offer the truth in such a way that it changes the whole person." [35]

Paul uses one of the greatest words in all the Bible in his second letter to Timothy to describe the Word of God—inspired. Literally, the verse (II Timothy 3:16) in the Greek New Testament begins, "The every written scripture is God-breathed..." It's almost beyond our comprehension to think within every copy of the Bible we hold are the words God breathed into men for His glory. Take note, these men were not stenographers simply taking dictation, like puppets with no mind of their own. God intentionally used the personality and perspective of each of the contributors of the Bible to speak to and through. The recorded words came through men, from God.

Probably the most significant aspect of the Bible's inspiration is the fact that the whole is so much more than just the sum of its parts. That's the way it is with anything involving the Lord. When God breathes, that into which He breathes is always more than the sum of its parts. When God breathed the breath of life into the nostrils of Adam, Adam became a living soul, not just the sum total of two eyes, two ears, two arms, and two legs. He was a complete being—mind, body, and soul—through God's inspired breath.

What this means is that when we say God breathed into the Bible, the sum total is infinitely more than just words—nouns, verbs, and adjectives randomly pieced together, recounting long ago history. The Bible is a living thing, capable of literally giving life! It lives because it is the Word of the living God.

I love the passionate description in "Ambassadors of God" of the rewards that come from delving into the Word: "One finds it well-nigh impossible to overestimate the joy of the golden hours you will devote to diligent study and the acquirement of Christian culture. Do not allow them to be filched away by lesser interests, nor permit yourselves to be taken out of the hands of the Sculptor who fashions His chosen servants and prepares them for their work." [36]

Whatever your words, your principles for preaching and teaching, your exhortations to your members, let it always flow from the Bible. It is the inerrant Word of God, the source of all truth, and abundantly able to meet every need we may encounter in all of life.

There is No Excuse for Being Unprepared to Preach

1

The high calling to preach is a 24-hours-a-day, 7-days-a-week calling. It is not for the weak, the weary, or those prone to fighting the battle of their will versus God's will. It is sacrificial service in its purest form, all in the name of Christ's Kingdom. Long before the constant assault of media and marketing, preachers were still faced with the many challenges of their calling.

More than 100 years ago, in "The Work of Preaching," Arthur S. Hoyt described the need of the church and the men called to serve her when he said, "The Church wants better men in her pulpits, not more men; prophets, not priests; the living word, not the professional repetition of truth. The noblest gifts, the richest furnishing, the best training, are not too much. But she must have men who shall regard preaching as the highest and most difficult art, who shall have lofty conceptions of it, who shall not be lazy or insincere, who shall bend themselves and hold themselves to its attainment." [37]

Most of the people you will serve will only see you in the pulpit, so always be prepared to give a word from God. Your congregation will most easily receive your word as you preach, so being prepared to share is your first priority of service to them. One of the most overlooked details in young pastor's careers is the amount of time necessary to prepare a worthy sermon. Most people discount the time and effort spent doing the research and rewriting and the polishing and perfecting, that it takes to prepare a sermon.

You will be well served from the beginning if you schedule non-negotiable blocks of time on your weekly calendar that you devote solely to your sermon. While some may be able to do it in less time, I found that it took me 25-30 hours every week to prepare my messages for my congregation. This was a practice I observed weekly for 35 years as a pastor.

For me, I found the mornings were the best and most productive time. I was fresh, alert, and made it a point to be in my study by 6:30 a.m. I found I could get more done in a few hours by beginning early than I could later in the day when distractions and interruptions almost always arose. There are considerably less demands of your time when you're at it and working long before most people have had their first cup of coffee.

Legendary pastor W. A. Criswell had a similar practice. He set up his study in his home and never left the house before noon, preferring instead to study in his pajamas. He said something as minor as dressing for the day could be done anytime, but his most productive time was early on and so he gave it to his study of the Lord.

Throughout my years of preaching, I have always enjoyed verse-by-verse sermons that focus on an individual book of the Bible. This made it easy to know where I was headed week by week. I could focus on the message for the week and know what was coming next week, too. Whenever I preached isolated passages or themes of the Bible, it took me more preparation time to research related verses and to make sure I was presenting them in their full context. Both kinds of sermons have their own merit, but I have found expository messages throughout a specific book will save you time in preparation in the long run. They also have the added benefit of providing a thread of continuity, one week to the next, for your members to follow.

Whatever and however you preach, the challenge to prepare is real and has been felt for generations. It is a balance of time spent in the Word, time spent in prayer, reflection, and research, as these men attest:

From W. W. Melton – "The fact that a man is divinely called into the ministry does not mean God will supply the message without careful study on the minister's part: nor does it imply that God will excuse a man when he come to his pulpit without a burning message, if the man has wasted his time in gadding about when he should have been studying."[38]

From Hershael W. York – "Our preparation, our diligence to study, our commitment to be better communicators does not discount the power of the Spirit, but instead expects it. Because we really believe that God can and will use us, we prepare the text, the sermon, and our own delivery skills so we are fit vessels for God to use."[39]

The message regarding your message is simple: preparation is essential; make it your top priority.

1 Don't Flirt with Temptation

Temptation comes at us in many forms. We're constantly bombarded by advertisements and signs to "do this," "try that," or "to live a little." Just the number of commercials on television alone is overwhelming, let alone billboards, radio ads, signs, marquees, and more. Everywhere you turn there are offers of temptation—few of which will ever bring honor and glory to God.

The men of Jesus' day were also tempted by many of the same temptations men of today's culture face. Though there were no red, neon signs flashing along the roadways, the opportunities for infidelity, overindulgence, and other shameful behavior remained just the same. That is probably why the apostles gave such strong advice in this area. Paul was clear and decisive in II Corinthians 4:2 when he said, "Instead, we have renounced shameful secret things, not walking in deceit or distorting God's message, but commending ourselves to every person's conscience in God's sight by an open display of truth."

The word 'renounced' speaks of a renunciation that was made at a specific point in time. It has the idea of refusing, disclaiming, giving up, to forbid, speak against, set forth, and declare a position. All of these words are relevant to a minister—especially when facing temptation. It is absolutely imperative for a minister of the Gospel to set clearly defined parameters of his life—both personal and public—if he is to be most effective. That is precisely what renunciations are.

Taken a step further, a renunciation means to forbid the approaching of things previously disowned or renounced. In other words, when we take a stand against something, it is a final and permanent decision to renounce these things and disown them. We will not consider them, approach them, or make room for them in our hearts and minds. We are taking an intentional stand against Satan and his snares.

One of the best examples of renunciation in my personal life pertains to my marriage. When I married Carol Ann, I pledged to be true to her throughout all our lives—not just when things were good or when I felt like it. Whenever I have been tempted with a moral compromise, I didn't have to decide whether to yield to it or not—I have already made that decision. I made a covenant commitment to her 59 years ago to be true to her for the rest of our lives and forevermore, I don't have to decide whether or not I will break that covenant with her. It's a done deal through and through.

We get in to trouble when we entertain the 'what ifs' of temptation or consider that we're the exception to the rules of moral behavior. However, if you can point to a specific point in time when you made a commitment to renounce these areas of temptation and compromise, not allowing them the slightest consideration, you will stand a much greater chance of remaining uncompromised.

The minister that succeeds in a life of unblemished integrity has almost certainly made some strong and ironclad renunciations along the way. Just as there is an east and a west, an up and a down, a positive and a negative, the effective minister affirms what is right and true and honorable and rejects what is not. The success of a preacher's impact is not just dependent upon his giftedness; it also depends upon the character he has to use these gifts.

Gifts without character are like a beautiful container with no contents—attractive on the outside, but of no praiseworthy use beyond that. This is also an appropriate way to describe the lure of pornography, on the Internet and elsewhere. This is one of the most important renunciations a preacher must make. The easy accessibility and lack of accountability make this sin so very insidious. I easily consider this one of the top temptations of the ministry today. For every man that resists, there are many more who don't. And for all who do give in, they always think no one will ever find out about them. Sadly, many are terribly mistaken. It is a rare month that goes by without me learning of at least one pastor that has succumbed, been discovered, and lost his livelihood as a result of internet pornography.

It is tragic and preventable. When you set clearly defined and stable parameters within your life, you are setting yourself up for your best chance of success. You are drawing a line in the sand that you will not cross and making a commitment to what you will and will not do. Don't wait until you are tempted to make such decisions. It is infinitely harder and the success rate is dismally lower. Decide now, while you're of clear mind, and you'll be well armed against the temptations that cross your path on a daily basis.

Be Careful in Your Contact with the Opposite Sex

1

Remember what Paul said about temptation earlier? Turns out this wasn't his first warning to Christ-followers about the importance of maintaining their moral integrity. See his words in I Corinthian 6:18-20: "Run from sexual immorality! 'Every sin a person can commit is outside the body.' On the contrary, the person who is sexually immoral sins against his own body. Don't you know that your body is a sanctuary of the Holy Spirit who is in you, whom you have from God? You are not your own, for you were bought at a price. Therefore glorify God in your body."

There is no area of your life that is more prone to compromise than this one. Carefully, carefully guard your ministry to the opposite sex. Don't place the burden on others—it is you whom you should not trust.

As a young pastor, I was faced with such a temptation. Since I had been saved as a young boy, I always thought there were some things I would never do. I grew from a normal boy into young manhood without getting into many of the problems that sometimes come with adolescence.

And then, without even realizing what was happening, my eyes were opened to how quickly compromise and temptation can take hold. A lady in our church began going out of her way to relate to me in subtle, yet personal ways. As her actions continued, I eventually realized that ours could develop into much more than just a pastoral relationship. I have to admit, I was infatuated with the idea and flattered by the attention she was giving me. But I knew I would never betray my marriage covenant.

Then one day at a pastors' meeting nearby, the speaker shared his testimony and brought a challenge to us. I don't even remember what the exact challenge was, but I do know at that moment it seemed as if God was opening up my heart for me to see inside. What I saw was the deep, deep darkness of my own heart and the understanding that there truly was no sin I would not commit!

My heart was broken and I began to weep. I excused myself from the table and drove myself back to the church, weeping all the way. My small staff immediately gathered around me to pray and I went home to share it with Carol Ann. She was my greatest source of strength then as she is now. I wept most of the next three days and didn't eat for a week. I had literally lost my appetite with the staggering realization that I was completely capable of every sin anyone else might ever commit. I was consumed with repentance and confession to the Lord for days afterward.

You are capable of the same thing. Don't ever trust yourself and always realize you desperately need God's presence within you at all times. Claim these words from I Corinthians and build your life upon it:

"No temptation has overtaken you except what is common to humanity. God is faithful, and He will not allow you to be tempted beyond what you are able, but with the temptation He will also provide a way of escape so that you are able to bear it"

–I Corinthians 10:13.

If the occasion occurs when you find others who have compromised, be especially on your guard as Paul points out, "Brothers, if someone is caught in any wrongdoing, you who are spiritual should restore such a person with a gentle spirit, watching out for yourselves so you won't be tempted" (Galatians 6:1).

I urge you never to visit another woman alone without your wife or a responsible third person present. My wife always accompanied me on visitations to other women's homes or in the hospital. She is and always has been my best defense against temptation and poor judgment. She has a remarkable ability to pick up on cues from other women and has always been able to help me steer clear of potential danger even when I didn't realize it. Regrettably, over the course of a career in ministry, counseling, and leadership, there will always come your way a few who will try to tempt you and compromise your integrity. A present and vigilant partner is your most valuable defense against this.

At your office, a clear glass window can help to make sure all visits are transparent and free of suspicion. If that's not an option, leave the door open whenever you meet with someone, whoever they may be. All too often, pastors learn the hard way that you don't have to be guilty to be hurt; you only have to be accused. It's a crazy fact of human nature, but most people are quick to believe the worst about those they respect most.

For many years, Rick Warren of Saddleback Church shared a message on purity with his staff and leadership team. I highly recommend it, but one of the key points stated that no man should ever ride on an elevator alone with a woman. And while that may seem a bit extreme, it was a simple precaution his ministry took to protect itself from temptations and accusations. Apparently the message took hold in the Saddleback culture as one day Rick approached the elevator the same time as a female staff member. She remembered the sermon and was quick to ask, "Well, do you ride first or do I?"

From the words of Paul to more contemporary men of God, know this—you can never be too careful in your dealings with the opposite sex. Do what you need to do to remove this temptation in advance and you'll never find yourself in a questionable situation.

Be an Example of Integrity

As a minister, it is imperative that you be a person of complete integrity. This means that you are the same person in private that you portray in public. Integrity is often described as the firm adherence to a code or standard of values and involves making good decisions that are consistent with the Word of God. Integrity also means always being truthful, maintaining wholesome moral character, and uprightness in all actions. To preach the truth, we must always live the truth!

Danny Akin explains what this looks like in practical terms in an article he wrote for Baptist Press called "Integrity in Ministry." He said, "The practice of honesty is more convincing than the profession of holiness. Let your words be true. Let them be kind and considerate. Let them be consistent with your faith in God." [40]

The Scripture also calls us to this kind of living. The Apostle Paul charged Timothy with these words, "'...you should be an example to the believers in speech, in conduct, in love, in faith, in purity'" (I Timothy 4:12).

Chuck Swindoll shared his views on integrity in "Rise and Shine," when he wrote, "Integrity evidences itself in ethical soundness, intellectual veracity, and moral excellence. It keeps us from fearing the white light of close examination and from resisting the scrutiny of accountability. It is honesty at all cost...rocklike character that won't crack when standing alone or crumble when pressure mounts." [41]

As pastors, we are most definitely NOT exceptions to the rules—especially in terms of integrity. The greatest tragedy for us as preachers of the Word is when we think that the commands of God are for others and not applicable to us. It is a subtle trap we can fall prey to when we begin to see ourselves as free from the very guidelines God's Word provides. When you live out what you preach, your character will be above reproach, and your reputation will be one of honesty and integrity.

Long-time leadership guru George Barna has always been unwavering in his call for steadfast integrity: "A leader's commitment to walk with integrity of heart calls for a refusal to allow even minor deviations from honesty of any kind... This is commitment to a healthy mind-set, a dedication to an 'inner-heart lifestyle' lived in the joy of God's grace and in the fullness of peace we are given in Christ." [42]

I've come to realize that words have a way of changing over time. For example, when Queen Elizabeth first saw St. Paul's Cathedral, accompanied by the architect himself, Sir Christopher Wren, these were her comments as she stood before the great altar: "It is awful, it is amusing, and it is artificial." In today's world, those would all be considered a terrible slam against what is one of the most beautiful structures in the world. However, the Queen's comments meant something completely different in 1710.

To say something was awful meant is was 'awe-full,' inspiring great awe—completely appropriate for the great cathedral. If something was considered amusing back then, it was worthy of one's 'musings' or thoughts—again, an accurate description of the cathedral. And finally, buildings and structures that were deemed artificial in the Queen's day meant they were 'artful' or stood as great works of art—an understatement, to say the least, regarding this magnificent building.

Similarly, the word 'character' has changed considerably—even in our own lifetimes. Originally, one of character indicated one had a central core of integrity or an unchanging concept of values that was virtually unshakeable. For individuals, it meant a consistency of life and behavior that was based upon integrity. In recent years, character has come to mean something much more cavalier, more colorful, and more closely related to one's personality and the temporary habits others see on display from time to time.

When I speak of character, it has nothing to do with shifting personality traits that can be subject to moods and circumstances; it has everything to do with that center of integrity that doesn't change no matter what. It is our plumb line, our North Star, our unmovable point of reference and basis of beliefs around which everything else in our life navigates. It is a core of stability that never wavers when everything else around it is swirling about. I like to think of it as the guard stationed at the gate to your heart, mind, and soul whose job is to screen every thought, temper every word, and control ever action. It is, without a doubt, the single most significant ingredient to long-term success. Without character, no other achievement will last.

Someone once stopped the world-famous conductor and pianist Paderewski, and asked him on a Manhattan street corner, "How do you get to Carnegie Hall?" His famous misunderstanding yielded the answer, "Practice, my friend, practice." Character is the sum total of a lifetime of practices that, indeed, add up to considerably more than the sum of its parts. Be sure that each of these practices is done with integrity!

1 Don't Fall into the Money Trap

I strongly urge you to have nothing to do with receiving or spending of the church's funds, including signing checks on the church's account. Always require two independent signatures for church checks and other withdrawals. And be extra wary of using credit cards, making sure to never use the church's card for personal items and always documenting church business expenses with a receipt. I realize sometimes it's easier to skip the record-keeping trouble of filing receipts, but I promise, it will always serve you well to abide by these wise financial practices.

Though money and benefits are naturally of concern when facing a decision to accept a position, they should never be your biggest interest. Be more interested in whether it is God's Will for you to accept the position than you are in your salary and benefits. The real issue for you must always be the will of God. If you are truly answering a call the Lord has placed upon your heart that should take precedence over any financial package or other incentives the budget committee offers.

I have never known what my salary would be in any church until I received my first paycheck, oftentimes weeks after I had accepted the offer. I'm not necessarily suggesting that you don't visit with members of the pastor search committee regarding your potential salary and benefits—I am just encouraging you to not let these discussions become a time of making demands. If God wants you there, He will take care of provisions for you and your family.

Whenever possible with your personal funds, make every effort to live without going into debt with the exception of a mortgage, if housing is not provided. Set your goal to become debt-free as soon possible so that you are not beholden to anyone for any possessions. For our family, it took a considerable amount of time to pay off long-standing debts—25 years after graduating from seminary. It was a slow, but steady process, and worth every sacrifice we made along the way. It was a momentous day when we finally had no other debt outside of our home. Maintaining an excellent credit rating and living debt-free are some tremendous examples of being wise stewards with the financial means the Lord provides for each of us. When you live like this, you are impacting others and setting a needed example for others to follow.

One of the devil's strongest and most persistent schemes is to destroy our credibility through our dealings with money. When we spend more than we have, want more than we have, or spend what we do have foolishly or not for the benefit of others, we allow Satan to establish a foothold that can soon become something more. As an example, don't ask for or expect special favors. Whether it is a reduced rate on your car repair or an extra percentage off your kid's piano lessons, don't ever get to the place where you expect special considerations.

Remember, any taxable gift given to you by the church must be valued at the time and reported to the IRS. You'll help yourself (and your accountant!) if you keep an ongoing record of significant gifts and their estimated value throughout the year. Come tax time, you can easily determine if and how much you owe in taxes.

I recall that, as an anniversary present from LifeWay, the trustees sent Carol Ann and me on an Alaskan cruise. And while we didn't have to pay for the trip, we did owe taxes based on the cost of the cruise. Likewise, when I retired, we received many, many gifts from the trustees and well-wishers. Always be cognizant that such gifts have to be documented, reported, and considered as income.

You are a Steward of Your Position and Influence

Whatever God has brought into your life and ministry is given to you as a stewardship. This is true for the successes you've enjoyed, failures and disappointments you've endured, challenges you've overcome, and lessons you've learned. The tapestry of your life, made up of good times and bad, revelations revealed, and paths forged can be of tremendous benefit to your peers, your church members, and the generation of preachers that will follow you.

Many pastors feel they are too busy to go to pastors' meetings or other conferences. The truth is that other pastors need the influence, support, and encouragement of long tenured and effective pastors. We are stewards of our influence and time as well as our physical possessions. If you're relatively new to the ministry, you'll benefit from the wisdom, encouragement, influence, and support of long-tenured and effective older pastors. And when you find yourself as one of the most experienced in the room, it's time to share and lead those coming after you. We are every bit as much stewards of our influence as we are of our possessions.

Again, the words from Rick Warren's "Purpose Driven Life" are completely appropriate here: "Our time on earth and our energy, intelligence, opportunities, relationships, and resources are all gifts from God that he has entrusted to your care and management. We are stewards of whatever God gives us." [43]

None of us can fulfill The Great Commission by ourselves—nor are we intended to. Even if each of our churches were to baptize thousands each year, we would hardly make a dent in the considerable gap between the lives won over for Christ and the constantly increasing population. That's not meant to discourage you by any means—quite the contrary! It's merely a simple statistic that can be swayed significantly when we use the compounding effect of area-wide churches working together, sharing our joint influence for the cause of the Gospel and the betterment of our communities.

When you pour your life into others, you are following the example the Lord set for each of us. In just a few years of ministry, Jesus poured His life, His lessons, and encouragements into a small band of men He chose to carry on with His message after He was gone. The most surprising thing about these men is that there was not a significant person in the lot! None of them could boast of upper class backgrounds, professional accomplishments, or advanced education. In fact, it was quite the opposite!

These men were working class at best, making their living as fishermen, tax collectors, and carpenters. They were unkempt, poor of speech, and most without any semblance of financial security. None of them were politically well connected, respected within their religion, or carried the honorable stature of say, a Pharisee, Sadducee, Herodian, or Roman. And none of them were suited to be a member of the ruling body, the Sanhedrin.

Consider the make-up of these first disciples as a testament to the changing power of Christ in a man's life:

- Peter cursed Christ and denied even knowing Him not once or twice, but three times all the while Christ was held captive;

- James and John, known as 'sons of thunder' were given to extreme fits of rage and anger and always holding onto their mother's apron strings in an effort to curry favor with Jesus;

- Phillip was clueless at best, always at a loss for what was going on around him;

- Matthew sold out his own people in order to become a tax collector, reporting to the occupying army of Rome. In today's equivalent, this would be much like an American aligning himself with ISIS.

- In contrast to Matthew, Simon the Zealot was known to slash and stab first, ask questions later; (Just the extreme difference between Matthew and Simon the Zealot must have made for pretty intense discussions).

- And finally, Thomas, the doubter to end all doubters who was suspicious of Christ's resurrection, and even the details of the crucifixion despite evidence to the contrary.

What a rag-tag, self-absorbed, self-seeking, competitive and clueless bunch of men that Christ called together to lay the foundation for His first church! The men represented the ills of society back then. They lacked any kind of dynamic communication skills. And they were the last you would suspect of carrying forth a compelling message.

And yet, they did.

In preaching to the Corinthians, Paul did his best to show how the saving grace of Christ could transform even the lowliest of men:

"Now we have this treasure in clay jars, so that this extraordinary power may be from God and not from us. We are pressured in every way but not crushed; we are perplexed but not in despair; we are persecuted but not abandoned; we are struck down but not destroyed" (II Corinthians 4:7-9).

Paul uses the metaphor of us as clay pots, saying we are charged with being stewards of the wonders of God and to always be found faithful: "...consider us in this way: as servants of Christ and mangers of God's mysteries. In this regard, it is expected of managers that each one of them be found faithful" (I Corinthians 4:1-2). Though we each are humbly and simply made, as believers, we each carry inside of us a treasure of gold. If we fall down, we must get up; if we fall behind, we must catch up. Ours is to be a journey of faith throughout our lives.

It is all too easy to attach unrealistic and unattainable attributes to what faithfulness means. It does not mean success or perfection. It is not equivalent to brilliance or flawlessness. It doesn't mean you won't fall or fail. Faithfulness means that, at the end of the day, a believing and Christ-filled man will get up, carry on, and deliver the treasure of the Gospel to others.

Let this be our constant prayer that when our race is run and our day is done, that it will be said we delivered the treasure of Christ's love to where we were sent.

Don't Be Surprised by Opposition

It is unrealistic to expect your tenure as a pastor to be without opposition at some point. It may be over visions for church growth, the actions of staff members, or even something as small as service times. But whether you're met with opposition for issues large or small, it still can cause considerable pain. That's because the people you love and have been called to serve disagree with you and see things differently than you. Frequently, they are vocal in their opposition and don't hesitate to share the opinions.

For me and many other pastors I've known, these challenges are usually marked by a season of deep darkness, but also times of tremendous growth. John Gossip shared a great perspective on these painful, yet beneficial, times in "The Hero in Thy Soul:" "Wordsworth tells us that his greatest inspirations had a way of coming to him in the night, and that he had to teach himself to write in the dark that he might not lose them. We, too, had better learn this art of writing in the dark. For it were indeed tragic to bear the pain, yet lose what it was sent to teach us." [44]

Keep in mind that whatever hurtful words or even mean-spirited actions we face, Christ faced much worse. He also warned us that, as committed Christians, we should expect to be criticized. He tells us this in John 15:20, "...If they persecuted Me, they will also persecute you."

Make every effort to respond to your critics with kindness. Be the example Christ was to his persecutors—not repaying evil for evil, but kindness for evil. Paul quoted Proverbs 25:21-22 as an example of this when he said, "... If your enemy is hungry, feed him. If he is thirsty, give him something to drink. For in doing you will be heaping fiery coals on his head. Do not be conquered by evil, but conquer evil with good" (Romans 12:20-21).

Your attitude, actions, and words towards opposition may not always produce the healing you are seeking, the resolution of the issue at hand, or even the restoration of the relationship, but God's Word calls us to respond in kindness. When you don't engage in hostile discussions or make disparaging remarks against those who challenge you, you can be confident you are standing on the truth of God's Word and bringing honor to Christ.

When you show love to all those you are called to serve and ask only that God's will be done, you will always please God, even if your opposition may not be pleased.

In the Book of Matthew, Jesus speaks directly to His followers, warning them of the persecution to come on account of Him:

"'Brother will betray brother to death, and a father his child. Children will even rise up against their parents and have them put to death. You will be hated by everyone because of My name. But the one who endures to the end will be delivered.'"

–Matthew 10:21-22

And again, a few verses later:

"Don't assume that I came to bring peace on earth. I did not come to bring peace, but a sword."

–Matthew 10:34

And the words of Paul to Timothy promising difficulties for believers:

> "...What persecutions I endured! Yet the Lord rescued me from them all. In fact, all those who want to live a godly life in Christ Jesus will be persecuted." – II Timothy 3:11-12

And finally, Peter had much to say about the opportunity for blessings and honor that oftentimes accompany the cost of standing for Christ:

> "And who will harm you if you are deeply committed to what is good? But even if you should suffer for righteousness, you are blessed. Do not fear what they fear or be disturbed, but honor the Messiah as Lord in your hearts. Always be ready to give a defense to anyone who asks you for a reason for the hope that is in you. However, do this with gentleness and respect, keeping your conscience clear, so that when you are accused, those who denounce your Christian life will be put to shame. For it is better to suffer for doing good, if that should be God's will, than for doing evil." –I Peter 3:13-17

> "Dear friends, don't be surprised when the fiery ordeal comes among you to test you as if something unusual were happening to you.

Instead, rejoice as you share in the sufferings of the Messiah, so that you may also rejoice with great joy at the revelation of His glory. If you are ridiculed for the name of Christ, you are blessed, because the Spirit of glory and of God rests on you…But if anyone suffers as a 'Christian,' he should not be ashamed but should glorify God in having that name." –I Peter 4:12-15, 16

That is a wonderfully uplifting outlook that helps us see the redeeming end to suffering for the cause. Christ tells us He suffered for those who would come after Him; He promises we will face opposition for our beliefs, too; and Peter proclaims the honor available to us in adversity. This is a 'glass half-full' perspective of heavenly stature!

Adrian Rogers had a unique perspective regarding our roles as leaders of the faith: "Be warned! From Satan's viewpoint you are a pawn in his game of cosmic chess. Plans have already been made in Satan's underworld to sabotage you, your loved ones, and your family. How does he plan to gain the upper hand over you? He uses two chief weapons— the world and the flesh. Together, with his orchestrations, they make up a trinity of evil—the world, the flesh, and the devil. They are interactive forces in a three-pronged attack." [45]

The threat of Satan bringing harm to my family and my church are serious fighting words! It makes me want to do everything within my power to defeat the enemy and protect them. If that means resisting the temptation to get even or not engaging in heated arguments with my most vocal opponents, or not reacting impulsively when confronted, I am all for fighting the battle with kindness and restraint.

Although we should expect opposition from those outside the faith—those who don't understand or strongly disagree with our beliefs, some of the most daunting challenges come from within our own church family—the people we call family and share our daily lives with. Undoubtedly, this is the most hurtful of conflicts. When you are attacked from within the church family, do everything you can to be reconciled with your detractors. Disharmony within the church is the very thing Jesus prayed about in His High Priestly prayer in John 17.

Just before leaving His disciples to return to His Father, Christ prayed for them, asking for unity among their ranks:

"'I am no longer in the world, but they are in the world, and I am coming to You. Holy Father, protect them by Your name that You have given Me, so that they may be one as We are one.'"

–John 17: 11

Christ knew there were already tensions and a tendency for divisiveness among His disciples. Some were jealous of James and John, some fought their own insecurities, and some were given to their own egos and mostly concerned with looking out for themselves. The fact that they had argued among themselves over who was the greatest only hours before gives so much insight into their self-absorption. It is no wonder Christ was concerned about the group's unity after He was gone and petitioned God to bring them together.

Beyond His immediate concerns, Christ was also focused on the unity of future generations and prayed fervently on their behalf later in the chapter:

> "'I pray not only for these, but also for those who believe in Me through their message. May they all be one, as You, Father, are in Me and I am in You. May they also be one in Us, so the world may believe You sent Me. I have given them the glory You have given Me. May they be one as We are One. I am in them and You are in Me. May they be completely one, so the world may know You have sent Me and have loved them as You have loved me.'" –John 17: 20-23

Christ was looking into the distant future, praying for those in distant lands and places and ages to come who would believe in Him. Because Jesus was asking God for unity, it proves that unity is something received, not achieved. It is not something we can accomplish; it is a divine gift, directly from God. Spiritual unity cannot, under any circumstances, be organized or manipulated by man. It can only be energized by the Spirit of God as He wills. No fabrication on the part of man will ever bring about spiritual unity. It is the Lord's work alone.

Christ gives us the pattern for this unique kind of unity. It is the unity between the Father and the Son and is the model and source for unity among us as believers. We are to strive for this model relationship one-to-another as well as corporately, between a pastor and his congregation. It is the gold standard against which we should measure all our relationships.

Expect opposition, but desire and seek to maintain unity. Though we can't create unity, we can work to protect and guard it as Paul told the Ephesians:

"Therefore I, the prisoner for the Lord, urge you to walk worthy of the calling you have received, with all humility and gentleness, with patience, accepting one another in love, diligently keeping the unity of the Spirit with the peace that binds us." –Ephesians 4: 1-3

Charles Stanley relates an incident that happened to him in his early days as pastor of First Baptist Church Atlanta. His opposition had been loud and aggressive and he was facing conflict from all sides. In the midst of this chaos, he received an invitation from an elderly lady in his congregation to her home for lunch. Overwhelmed with confusion swirling around him, he almost declined, but at the last minute, accepted and went to her home.

After lunch she led him into another room to look at a picture on her wall. It was a picture of Daniel in the lion's den looking up to heaven. She asked him what he saw in the picture. He mentioned several things, but not what she wanted him to see. When he asked what he was missing she told him, "Daniel was not looking at the lions!"

By keeping his sights heavenward, Daniel wasn't distracted by the threats of those nearby; he was too focused on God to be concerned with the lions about him. It's a great metaphor to represent how we are to react when conflicts arise. Expect opposition, but don't focus on the lions in your life.

You Can't Please Everyone!

Trying to please everyone is impossible. No matter how hard you try, what stance you take or what project you support, it is quite literally impossible to please everyone. There will always be some who feel slighted or overlooked; some will be resentful, others will feel compromised or used. If a consensus is required from a crowd of two or more, there will always be those displeased.

The whole exercise in even trying to please everyone is futile and frustrating. And the end result is usually the same: you end up pleasing no one after all your efforts. This is especially true in the life of a pastor.

Most of us desire to be accepted and respected by others. We all crave the approval of others. Pastors are no different. And while most pastors don't set out to make others angry or become belligerent towards them, it is all too easy to do so when we fall into the trap of trying to please everyone.

You're probably familiar with Aesop's Fables—legendary fables that usually carried with them a moral lesson learned at the expense of the characters. One of my favorites is "The Man, the Boy, and the Donkey," and it goes like this:

"A Man and his son were once going with their Donkey to market. As they were walking along by its side a countryman passed them and said: "You fools, what is a Donkey for but to ride upon?"

So the Man put the Boy on the Donkey and they went on their way. But soon they passed a group of men, one of whom said: "See that lazy youngster, he lets his father walk while he rides."

So the Man ordered his Boy to get off, and got on himself. But they hadn't gone far when they passed two women, one of whom said to the other: "Shame on that lazy lout to let his poor little son trudge along."

Well, the Man didn't know what to do, but at last he took his Boy up before him on the Donkey. By this time they had come to the town, and the passers-by began to jeer and point at them. The Man stopped and asked what they were scoffing at. The men said:

"Aren't you ashamed of yourself for overloading
   that poor donkey of yours and your hulking son?"

The Man and Boy got off and tried to think what to do. They thought and they thought, till at last they cut down a pole, tied the donkey's feet to it, and raised the pole and the donkey to their shoulders. They went along amid the laughter of all who met them till they came to Market Bridge, when the Donkey, getting one of his feet loose, kicked out and caused the Boy to drop his end of the pole. In the struggle the Donkey fell over the bridge, and his forefeet being tied together he was drowned.

"That will teach you," said an old man who had followed them:

Please all, and you will please none." [46]

One of the greatest challenges you will face as a minister is the pressure to keep everybody happy at the same time. More often than not, it simply isn't possible. If you keep in mind that your first allegiance is always to obey God, it makes handling criticism and controversy a bit easier. If, in your heart, you know you are doing what is right and honorable before the Lord, you needn't allow your critics to bring you down.

Follow the lead of Peter and John who, when facing some of the strongest opponents to early Christianity, said, "...'Whether it's right in the sight of God for us to listen to you rather than to God, you decide; for we are unable to stop speaking about what we have seen and heard'" (Acts 4:19-20).

As pastor of one of the largest churches in the country, Rick Warren knows the difficulty in trying to please a large audience made up of all ages, all diversities, all socioeconomic standings, and all kinds of backgrounds. He determined early on that pleasing everyone was not even something worth considering: "I don't know all the keys to success, but one key to failure is to try to please everyone. Being controlled by the opinions of others is a guaranteed way to miss God's purposes for your life. Jesus said, 'No one can serve two masters.'" [47]

If a man who pastors tens of thousands has determined the futility of trying to please everyone, it's a safe bet we can learn from his wisdom and apply the same practice. You will not, nor should you, try to please everyone. Your goal is to please God in all you say and think and do.

If you are able to do this throughout your ministry, you will be able to affirm to God as Hezekiah did, "...'Please, Lord, remember how I have walked before You faithfully and wholeheartedly, and have done what pleases You...'" (Isaiah 38:3).

1 Be Quick to Forgive Mistakes

Mistakes are great teaching tools. We usually learn far more from our mistakes than we do our successes. They're a great way of learning what not to do, what not to say, or how not to handle certain situations. Because most of us by the time we're adults go well out of our way to avoid making mistakes, it important to show kindness and understanding when others falter and be quick to offer forgiveness.

When preaching to the Ephesians, Paul was emphatic about following Christ's example and extending forgiveness when he said, "'And be kind and compassionate to one another, forgiving one another, just as God also forgave you in Christ'" (Ephesians 4:32).

The Lord was also clear on all matters of forgiveness. In Matthew, in the Sermon on the Mount, He said, "'And forgive us our debts, as we also have forgiven our debtors'" (Matthew 6:12).

Then He continued, "'For if you forgive people their wrongdoing, your heavenly Father will forgive you as well. But if you don't forgive people, your Father will not forgive your wrongdoing'" (Matthew 6: 14).

Seems to be a straightforward set of expectations: do this, get that; don't do this, don't get that—directly from the Lord, no less. Forgiveness begets forgiveness. We all need it and we all need to extend it.

Usually, whenever I'm faced with someone who has made a mistake—no matter how egregious—I ask the person, "Did you do that on purpose?" They know I know otherwise and usually break into a smile. It softens the fallout from the mistake and lets them know I am on their side.

One of the many times I've used this tactic was on a business trip. My connecting flight was cancelled and I had to wait close to an hour just to make the arrangements to catch a flight home. When the ticket agent realized my status as a high-ranking frequent flyer, he began to apologize for the lengthy delay. When I asked him, "Did you do that on purpose," a smile broke out on his face and I reassured him, "Then, it's OK."

Another time, I had not been at my position at the Sunday School Board, now LifeWay, very long when I received a call from one of the technicians in our recording and satellite area. At the time, we had one of the only direct links to satellites in Nashville and many people rented our production equipment for their recordings. Long before I became president of LifeWay, Hank Williams, Jr. had become a regular client.

The technician who called me was clearly nervous about an incident that had happened earlier in the day. "I need to tell you something," he said. Hank, Jr. had been in to do some video recording and had it sent on to be placed on the air. The problem was that his recording violated some of our longstanding and strict guidelines about what could and could not be promoted using our facilities. He knew the guidelines and had chosen to violate them anyway.

The technician recounted what had happened that day. Because they were recording video and sending it out immediately, nothing could be changed or deleted once the video was shot. In the middle of Hank Jr.'s recording, he began to promote his upcoming Budweiser Beer-sponsored concert tour. The promotion of a brewery by someone using our facilities was a blatant violation of our policy, yet once the words were spoken, they couldn't be retrieved.

When the technician finished telling about it, I was quick to ask, "Well, did you let this happen on purpose?" He quickly and emphatically replied, "NO!" and that was all I needed to hear. I then told him, "Then it was beyond your control. Just don't let it happen again and know that I'll take the heat for it."

Be quick to forgive mistakes and use it as a chance to encourage others not to make the same mistake again. There's rarely a reason to be hostile towards others when they do make mistakes, so always err on kindness. Remember, you will need forgiveness and correction along the way, too.

As a follow-up, just a few weeks later I received a call from one of our trustees who had read an article about Williams' Budweiser Beer Tour. Included in the article was a picture of him with a sign behind him on the television that said, "Baptist Sunday School Board." A few phone calls later we had set the record straight about the relationship and our technician got a good lesson in leadership by watching someone else taking the blame for an innocent mistake. It's good to remember that no one makes mistakes on purpose!

Don't Quit Before You Finish

2

Christian Leadership is Being a Servant

2

Servant Leadership is the Key

At the heart of Christian leadership is service. Service to Christ. Service to fellow believers. Service to an unbelieving world. If a leader professes to be a Christian, he must have the heart of a servant to be his most effective.

In "Being Leaders" by Aubrey Malphurs, he described it like this: "Christian leaders are servants with the credibility and capabilities to influence people in particular context to pursue their God-given direction...Christian leadership is the process whereby servants use their credibility and capability to influence people in a particular context to pursue their God-given direction." [48]

When we speak of Christian leadership or ministry, we need to remember that it is not about authority, but influence, and this influence carries with it a tremendous responsibility. It is not a relationship based on a dictatorship, but servant hood. The Bible is full of examples of leadership models, beginning with our ultimate example, Jesus. Leading others along their life's journeys is a right that is best seen when we serve those whom God places in our path. As long as we begin and end with Jesus as our role model for Christian leadership, we will continue to broaden our influence and strengthen our impact.

John MacArthur wrote one of the most definitive books on Christian leadership, "The Book on Leadership." In it he says, "When people are convinced you will do everything in your power for their good and nothing for their harm, they'll trust you...All leadership begins there. A leader is not someone who is consumed with his own success and his own best interests. A true leader is someone who demonstrates to everyone around him that their interests are what most occupy his heart." [49]

If the very essence of your ministry is being a servant to others, there isn't room for power struggles, exercises in exerting authority, or the search for prestige. It is about serving people and leading people with a heart of love and compassion. It is about leading people without driving them; building personal relationships through personal contact; and about demonstrating the very principles you are trying to instill in others. There is no place for dictatorial or arbitrary behavior in Christian leadership.

The Apostle Paul found himself right in the middle of a power struggle when he was dealing with the church in Corinth. Division and controversy consumed the church, much of it centered around the leadership. In the very first chapter of I Corinthians, Paul says,

"Now, I urge you, brothers, in the name of our Lord Jesus Christ, that all of you agree in what you say, that there be no divisions among you, and that you be united with the same understanding and same conviction. For it has been reported to me about you, my brothers, by members of Chloe's household, that there is rivalry among you. What

I am saying is this: Each of you says, 'I'm with
Paul,' or 'I'm with Apollos,' or 'I'm with Cephas,' or
'I'm with Christ.'" – I Corinthians 1:10-12

Whatever the intentions of those involved, God never
intended for Christian leadership to be a matter of conflict.

By the third chapter, Paul is accusing the people of the
Corinthian church as being "babies in Christ" (I Corinthian
3:1), succumbing to envy and strife among themselves and
being "fleshly...and living like unbelievers..." (I Corinthians
3:3). What an insult that must have been as it would be for
us—to be accused of living as unbelievers. He then continues,
"What then is Apollos? And what is Paul? They are servants
through whom you believed, and each has the role the Lord
has given" (I Corinthians 3:5). Pay close attention to what he
is asking. He doesn't ask *who* Apollo is or **who** Paul is; he asks
what Paul and Apollos are and then he proceeds to explain
what their role is as servants.

The word translated 'servants' is the same word from
which we get the word 'deacon' and is used to refer to a
common servant, one who will do the most menial task
asked of him for the benefit of those in need. This speaks of
a servant spirit, free of arrogance or any sense of domination.
It was frequently used to refer to someone who has
distinguished himself through active and ongoing service to
others. It was also another word for waiter. Paul and Apollos
were not church CEOs or hard-driving achievers motivated

by bottom line goals. On the contrary, they were known as **diakonoi**, servants of God and serving others.

In Luke 22:27, Jesus describes Himself with the same word. It speaks precisely to this great need for humility among authentic Christian leaders. Adrian Rogers addressed this in his book, "The Incredible Power of Kingdom Authority," when he says, "The pastor's leadership is servant leadership. The pastor is first a servant and then a leader. Any pastor not under authority has forfeited his right to exercise authority. Jesus is the sovereign Lord of the church, but notice his method of loving leadership. 'I am among you as he that serveth' (Luke 22:27). This truth ought to make it clear that the pastor is not a boss or a dictator. God's sheep are not to be driven or herded but led by a loving shepherd." [50]

Unbelievably, in just a few verses prior to this at the celebration of the Passover meal, the disciples were clearly more concerned with their own welfare than the significance of what was about to take place. Moments after the Lord offered the bread and wine in remembrance of Him, the disciples resumed their discussion: "Then a dispute also arose among them about who should be considered the greatest" (Luke 22: 24). As incredibly inappropriate as their behavior is at such a significant time, every day we do much the same thing: wavering between giving the Lord the full glory and honor due him versus fighting for what or how we want things. The temptations of man have not changed significantly in the last 2,000+ years.

To study the lives of the disciples, you have to remember they were a rag-tag group of peasants, many of whom lived on the outskirts of a tiny lakeside village, far from any major city. Whether intrigued by His message or the compelling nature of Jesus, these men had put their lives on hold and abandoned their livelihoods to follow this itinerant, penniless preacher around for three years. Yet, here they were, on the eve of the greatest sacrifice in the history of the world, arguing about who was greatest, most accomplished, most honorable among themselves. The crazy thing is, they actually enjoyed this sort of argumentative banter and had held these discussions before! (Luke 9:46-48).

Jesus quickly put these discussions to rest by rebuking the disciples and saying, "'For who is greater, the one at the table or the one serving? Isn't it the one at the table? But I am among you as the One who serves'" (Luke 22:27).

The word 'servant' Jesus used is the same one Paul chose in I Corinthians when he described himself as a common servant, willing to do whatever was necessary for those whom He served. Jesus set the example for all of us who would follow His call into the ministry. He said it and He lived it and expected those who came after him to realize Christian ministry equals servant leadership.

Christ showed his servanthood by washing the disciples' feet at the Passover meal in the upper room. John 13 vividly describes that selfless act. He was teaching that genuine service ignores the usual arguments about greatness. There is no place for selfish motives and self-promotion when you are serving for the Lord. Consider these two verses that confirm that:

> "'You call Me Teacher and Lord. This is well said, for I am. So if I, your Lord and Teacher, have washed your feet, you also ought to wash one another's feet. For I have given you an example that you also should do just as I have done for you.'" –John 13: 13-15

> "But He said to them, 'The kings of the Gentiles dominate them, and those who have authority over them are called 'Benefactors.' But it must not be like that among you. On the contrary, whoever is greatest among you must become like the youngest, and whoever leads, like the one serving.'" –Luke 22:25-26

It's hard to imagine wanting to wash someone else's feet when you just wrapped up a heated discussion about whom among you was greatest. Jesus knew this. That's why He was so intentional about not engaging in the usual petty chatter that men debated about themselves.

Jesus also knew that genuine service bypasses the usual excuses for serving others: not enough time, hurtful feelings or jealousy, limited resources. He knew none of these excuses were reason enough not to embrace Christian service to others as the most effective way of advancing Christianity.

Despite the bickering among the disciples, Jesus knew His hour had come for Him to return to the Father. He knew Judas Iscariot was going to betray him, and He most certainly knew that God had delivered all authority into His hands. If ever there was someone with ample excuses, Jesus Christ was the one. He could have defaulted to one of several legitimate excuses why it was not suitable that He should serve His disciples on any level.

And yet He didn't.

In light of the circumstances—grown men arguing about whom among them was greatest in the very presence of the Living God...and on the eve of His crucifixion, no less!—Jesus did the most humbling thing possible—He washed their feet. It is almost unfathomable the depth of the humility of what Christ did for His disciples. He stooped before them, washed the dirtiest and most lowly part of their bodies, and carefully dried them with His servant's towel. The magnitude of this incredible act is still reverberating throughout history and still serving as the example of self-less, sacrificial love.

Jesus also showed the importance of serving when others neglect to serve. At the beginning of the Passover celebration on Thursday at sunset, the disciples quietly entered the Upper Room where Jesus had invited them to share what was to be His last meal. Disgruntled and still simmering from their arguments regarding their self-proclaimed greatness, it's safe to say few, if any, were in the right frame of mind to wash one another's feet. This was the perfect opportunity for Jesus to show the honor of service when others refuse. And He did so without so much as a word of condemnation, preferring to let His actions make the statement. He shows us it always helps to remember that someone else's failure is an opportunity for faithful service, not criticism.

One of the strongest statements Christ's action made were to show that real servants act even when those they serve are undeserving. Obviously, these men did not deserve the humble act of Christ washing their feet. They were consumed with thoughts about themselves—their arrogant, contentious, and thoughtless selves. The impact comes because He served them in spite of their unworthiness.

Jesus was showing the men who were to carry on His ministry after He was gone that a real servant acts in spite of ample reasons not to serve. Because the time had come for Him to go to the Father, He wanted to give them a lasting image of true servanthood. He knew that the Father had put all things under His power, because He had come from God and was to return to God—that is why He washed the disciples feet.

It is almost beyond comprehension that the One given absolute authority over all of mankind was the One who performed the most lowly service—washing the feet of the men who were called to carry the Gospel forward.

Again, Rick Warren gives a great explanation of Christ's love in "The Purpose Driven Life:" "The world defines greatness in terms of power, possessions, prestige, and position…Jesus, however, measured greatness in terms of service, not status. God determines your greatness by how many people you serve, not how many people serve you." [51]

Jesus also revealed that a real servant acts in spite of distractions in the midst of service. Again, if anyone ever had an excuse from service because of distractions, it was Jesus. Following the Passover Feast, Jesus was faced with two overwhelming distractions: His hour had come to be crucified and He was about to be betrayed by one of his disciples.

This was no new news to him—He lived His entire life with the crushing knowledge that He was going to be called upon to give His life for an undeserving, disrespecting, and selfish lot of people. What makes His service of washing the disciples' feet so staggering is that He did it in the face of the knowledge He was about to be betrayed, arrested, scourged, and crucified.

Jesus was facing a torturous death, the degrading march to the hill where He would die, and the disrespect of his executioners all the while knowing a personal betrayal was about to happen. In the face of an all-out betrayal from one He had shepherded so much, Jesus had every reason in the world to not serve his betrayer, Judas Iscariot. Instead, in the ultimate act of servitude, Jesus knelt and washed the feet of the man who would turn Him over to His executioners.

The spirit of Christ would have us serve the very ones we hold in the most contempt. What a revival that would be if this were to happen in the church!

Another of the hallmarks of genuine service is a willingness to act on an immediate need—not when circumstances are comfortable for you and your schedule. Jesus knew His time had come, yet still He acted when He saw the need. In the simple act of washing their feet, Jesus was leaving the disciples with an unforgettable example of true and sacrificial love for them to carry on: "Before the Passover Festival, Jesus knew that His hour had come to depart from this world to the Father. Having loved His own who were in the world, He loved them to the end" (John 13:1). In the case of the Passover dinner, the real need once the disciples took their place at the table was dirty feet! These men had trudged through the day, probably in leather sandals, and their feet were showing the effects of the day.

True service of the heart also takes the initiative. From what we know of the Last Supper from John's meticulous records, the meal had begun and the men's feet should have already been washed. Since no one else had taken the initiative, Jesus got up from the meal, removed His outer garments and doubtless stripped to nothing more than a loincloth—the clothing of a true slave. The long towel He tied around His waist for drying the disciples' feet was also in line with how a slave usually acted.

Possibly one of the most wonderful aspects of authentic Christian service is that it always has a fuller significance than just the moment at hand. In this case, the thoughts and priorities of Jesus and His disciples were vastly different.

Although Jesus knew the tremendous significance of what He was doing, the disciples had no clue, even Peter who argued with Him about washing his feet: "Jesus answered him, 'What I'm doing you don't understand now, but afterward you will know'" (John 13:7).

Jesus knew they would gain knowledge of what He was doing by slow experience and that they would come to realize the One who laid aside His garments would also lay aside His life; the One who washed their feet with water would wash away their sins with the blood of His Cross. Every act of Christian service points away from and beyond itself to the ultimate act of service on the Cross.

We have before us a needy and hurting world. With salvation in our hearts, the towel of service in our hand, Christ dwelling within us, and the Father exalted above us, we have within us the power to impact the world for Christ. In "Spiritual Leadership," Henry and Richard Blackaby explain this calling: "Jesus established the model for Christian leaders. It is not found in his 'methodology.' Rather, it is his absolute obedience to the Father's will...Spiritual leaders understand God is their leader." [52]

Richard Foster, author of "Celebration of Discipline," makes a great distinction between serving and being a servant. In an article he wrote for "Christianity Today," Foster says, "When we choose to serve we are still in charge. We decide whom we will serve and when we will serve. But when we chose to be a servant, we give up the right to be in charge. There is great freedom in this. When we choose to be a servant we surrender the right to decide who and when we will serve. We become available and vulnerable." [53]

Foster's distinction is more than just a little convicting. It is so very easy to serve without truly being a servant, but we are called to be servants of God's people, to God's people, in all that we do and say. That means we are to be accessible to those around us. We are called to listen to them, celebrate with them, cry with them, and comfort them. When we are servants in our community, it spills out in the way we treat the clerk at the grocery store or the dry cleaners or your waiter at a restaurant. Every exchange with others is an opportunity for us to be a servant.

I love the way Pat MacMillan presents the true heart of servant leadership in "The Performance Factor:" "Leaders who must rely on positional authority and autocratic style to achieve their ends seldom see the levels of performance shown to leaders who see their role as one of service and support...Servant leadership is much more an attitude than a skill...the key to becoming a servant leader is to see leadership as a role from which to serve, not a position to be served." [54]

Christian leadership equates to service with a servant's heart. It is not concerned with titles or rank, power or prestige. It is focused on speaking Jesus into the hearts and souls of those we encounter every day, in every way.

2

Be Open and Honest

It is important that people see you as a "real" person, not someone whose only presence is preaching from the pulpit. Make every effort to make sure the person you are in public is the same one you are in private. It is worth the risk to be transparent. Although some people may take advantage of your vulnerability, it is ultimately the key to effective ministry. Don't let your preaching voice be different than your everyday voice and God will use you as He made you. He intentionally made you as you are—don't try to create a new persona for the 'public' you.

In "Leadership for the 21st Century," Ron Boehme reinforces this idea: "Servant leadership is based on absolute truth and honesty. Righteous leadership flows from the heart of the leader who has been honest with himself about his true sinful condition, and has submitted his life to the mercy and transforming power of Jesus Christ. Openness and transparency give him the ability to be honest in all areas of life. He is able to live a life of humility and integrity as God gives him grace and guidance. He does not pretend to be someone he is not." [55]

William Mitchell in "Winning in the Land of the Giants," makes a strong case for being our most authentic selves when serving for the Lord: "The Lord made you with a set of fingerprints that are unique. Nobody else has them. Only you...You are somebody unique with a never-before-made body. The Lord made you with a history that nobody else has. He put you in a distinctive time and place in history, and He has given you a one-of-kind sequence and series of experiences in your life. You are somebody unique with a never-before-lived-past, present, and future. The Lord made you with a set of abilities, talents, gifts, and potentialities that nobody else has in precisely the same combination and degree." [56]

The highest compliment I've ever received comes from my children who have all at one point or another, said, "Dad was the same at home as he was in the pulpit." My family knows me best and knows the 'me' so many used to see on Sunday mornings was the same 'me' on Monday afternoon playing football with my boys. Honor the 'you' the Lord made you to be and don't waste time trying to be someone— anyone!—else.

When I went to First Baptist Dallas to serve as the Associate Pastor under the legendary Dr. W. A. Criswell, I had the opportunity to preach every Sunday evening and the mornings when he was gone. Because Dr. Criswell had such a presence and could silence an auditorium with his thunderous voice, I was frequently asked if preaching on Sunday nights, with him sitting right beside me, made me nervous or intimidated me.

When I replied, "No, it does not intimidate me," people were usually surprised, considering Dr. Criswell's impressive presence. And then I would go on to explain, "It did not take me but a week to realize I was not W. A. Criswell and could never be him. But I realize that I am the very best Jimmy Draper God ever made and all God expects of me is to be myself." It explained my perspective and gave them something to think about, too.

(I have to add that Dr. Criswell was my biggest fan and always gave me great encouragement when I preached. After I preached my first sermon at First Baptist Dallas, I asked him, "Pastor, you were nervous for me tonight, weren't you?" He chuckled and replied, "Ah lad, I did want you to succeed.")

Always remember you were uniquely created by God, for God. He wants—expects! you to use the gifts and personality He planted within you. You are at your best when you are not trying to become someone else. If you will just be who God created you to be, He will, most assuredly, take care of the rest!

2 Always Respond When People Contact You

If people reach out to you, it is your responsibility to respond to them in a timely manner. This means returning phone calls, sending emails, and drafting hard copies for regular mail. It may seem like a small thing to you—especially when so many ask so much of you—but I can assure you, a prompt response means considerably more to those contacting you. This discipline of making timely responses will reward you greatly, sharpen your disciplines in other areas, and enhance your relationships with those around you. No matter how full your schedule, do everything you can to return phone calls, emails, and letters promptly. When you fail to do so, you are communicating to the individuals involved that they're not important enough to warrant your time and attention.

As president of LifeWay, I initiated several practices that showed our staff just how important I considered prompt and personal communication with our customers. I insisted every phone call be answered within 24 hours at the most. And every letter had to be responded to within five business days since most involved a reference to a piece of literature and required some research. I also asked that no form letters be sent out as responses to often-asked questions. I wanted each and every letter to be personal enough so that the recipient knew we were responding to their individual letter. I felt so strongly about this basic common courtesy of quick replies that I received copies of every response that was sent out during my presidency.

With over 60 years involved in the public ministry, I have made it a practice to maintain these same standards in all my business and private communication. Just recently, a friend called with the tragic news concerning the death of his brother. Because we have maintained a strong relationship through visits, phone calls, emails, and postal mail, and I have responded to him promptly for the 30+ years of our friendship, I was the first call he made when he learned the news. Days after his phone call, I received an email from him that simply said, "Thanks for always being there for us."

You simply cannot afford to have the reputation that not everyone who contacts you is important enough to receive a timely reply. That completely contradicts what Jesus taught regarding our kindness and respect towards others. The brief moment it takes to make a phone call or send an email can serve to answer a question, provide much needed information, or give instruction, but beyond all this, it can deepen a relationship in small, incremental ways that build one upon the other over time. Don't underestimate the potential your responses can have on others in all sorts of ways. Every contact we have with others is an opportunity to express love, care, concern, and prayers. When we keep this in mind, we encourage others and please God.

2 We Need Each Other!

None of us can fulfill the Great Commission by ourselves. None!

The Southern Baptist 'distinctive of cooperation' is the best way to express your faithfulness to your calling. I experienced this first hand after serving in several top leadership positions. The year after I was president of the Southern Baptist Convention, I was vice-chairman of the Tarrant Baptist Association Executive Board. And even though the chairman of this board was a pastor who had once been my intern, I never once considered that I had taken a step down since the essence of what we were all working for and towards was cooperation. If we were to promote the health and effectiveness of churches and that was dependent upon cooperation, we certainly had to 'practice what we preached' and work in cooperation with one another.

Since the beginning, the Southern Baptist Convention has been based upon voluntary cooperation. The earliest Baptist associations began in England in the 17th-century and were formed to accomplish together what they could not accomplish alone. These associations involved both missions and evangelism as well as provided a chance for fellowships among churches and to preserve doctrinal integrity.

The theme of unity among believers originated from Christ. Throughout His prayer in John 17, Christ prays for unity/cooperation for all of His disciples, including the churches that would be born long after He was gone. His prayer was that they would come together as one heart and one mind. With the horrors of the cross immediately before Him, Jesus asked God to grant one great gift to His people: unity. Time after time, He asked God to give vital, spiritual unity to His followers. Seven times throughout this prayer He asked His Father to make His followers 'one.' On the eve of His death, Christ prayed for the 11 disciples as well as those believers to come:

"I pray not only for these,
but also for those who believe in Me
through their message.
May they all be one,
As You, Father, are in Me and I am in You.
May they also be one in Us,
So the world may believe You sent Me."

–John 17: 20-21

On the eve of his death, Jesus was looking to the future and praying for the generations that would follow Him, that they would come to know of His saving grace and desire a relationship with Him throughout their lives. He could actually look out at the masses and see a long line of believers who would be saved in the future. When He looked at Peter, He saw behind him the thousands at Pentecost who had believed. Looking at John, He saw the church at Ephesus and those in Roman Asia. Looking at the blank space where Judas had been, He saw Saul of Tarsus who changed his name to Paul and eventually became the Apostle Paul, and all the churches in Europe and the eventual spreading of the Gospel throughout the churches of Europe.

At this precise moment in time, Christ's gaze extended beyond the here and now and the real and the tangible. From Christ's viewpoint, He could see across the oceans and into the centuries to come. And he saw a multitude of believers— so many so, that man could never count them. His vision was so vivid and precise, He actually used the present tense of the verb as He spoke of future believers:

> "'I pray not only for these, but also for those who believe in Me through their message.'"
>
> –John 17: 20

It was as if, on the eve of His death, Christ was concerned for us—His future followers. Jesus was consciously praying for believers past, present, and future.

It is impossible for the Gospel to be fully effective in any group or congregation where there is a lack of unity among believers. Jesus prayed specifically for unity among His followers because He knew believers at odds with one another could never represent His unconditional love for others. He knew discord among His followers spoke louder than any gospel they preached and prayed accordingly:

> "'May they all be one,
> as You, Father, are in Me and I am in You.
> May they also be one in Us,
> so the world may believe You sent Me.
> I have given them the glory You have given Me.
> May they be one as We are one.
> I am in them and You are in Me.
> May they be made completely one,
> so the world may know You have sent Me
> and have loved them as You have loved Me.'"
>
> –John 17: 21-3

If we, as Christians, act in unity and cooperation with one another, the world will see that Jesus is the One God has sent to redeem the world.

The world cannot be evangelized by competing churches and personalities. No prayer of our Lord's has been so prevented from being answered by individual believers and by churches than this one. The Trinity demonstrates that God does not exist in splendid isolation, but that He is an associative God who uses relationships to best further His Kingdom. He fully expects and deserves for His followers to work in harmony together for His cause.

2 Build Strong Relationships

No one leads a successful life today without strong and far-reaching relationships. Having a strong and dynamic team of friends and family to support and encourage you, a vast network of contacts across all vocations, and committed and conscientious coworkers are the key to your achievement in the ministry. Without them, you are severely limited as to what you can accomplish and whom you can reach. *Everyone* in ministry needs the support of others.

In I Corinthians, Chapter 3, Paul discusses the need to partner with Apollos in order to reap a successful harvest of believers:

"'I planted, Apollos watered, but God gave the growth. So then neither the one who plants nor the one who waters is anything, but only God who gives the growth. Now the one planting and the one watering are one in purpose, and each will receive his own reward according to his own labor. For we are God's coworkers..."

–I Corinthians 3:6-9

Paul readily recognized his need for Apollos to come and water where he had planted. Had Apollos not partnered with Paul, the seed would have withered and died. These men were not competing isolationists, but rather synergistic coworkers. Their partnership presents a great illustration of working alongside, *not over*, our staffs, lay support team, friends, and family. The strongest relationships occur when there is mutual respect between two parties. Be careful not to dwell in some unapproachable ministerial ivory tower, situated physically and relationally well above your fellow servants. You will make the most progress and effective impact on Christ's Kingdom when you plant and water beside your fellow pastors.

Along the coast of northern California, the Coastal Redwoods have grown for centuries to create a sort of heavenly cathedral of trees, some reaching up to 365 feet high! One thing you can't help but notice is that these trees grow relatively close to one another. None of the ones who have lived for centuries have done it in isolation. (Life expectancy of Redwoods is 2,500 years!) And there's a very good reason for this: They need one another—for support, for protection, for they are strongest when they are together.

You see, redwoods don't have deep roots, especially considering their great height. Most of these mighty trees actually have very shallow roots and without the protection provided by their neighboring trees, they could not survive the strong coastal winds and torrential rainstorms of their region. As they grow upward, their roots become more and more entangled with nearby trees to the point where they are quite literally, inseparable. The trees actually hold one another up through their connected root systems. This symbiotic relationship with each other allows them to survive forest fires, pounding storms, gale-force winds, and other challenges. These magnificent trees reach great heights because they serve one another.

You will need a support system like that of the redwoods if you are to last in the ministry. Pastors that isolate themselves from their staffs or members or professional peers will burn out without the support of others. For those that do try to go it alone, they usually become bitter and jaded and cynical old men without having made a significant impact on the world.

Make every effort to stand by your brothers in the ministry. Meet with them regularly, attend conferences with them, and pray **with** and **for** them. Be the catalyst that organizes events that bring pastors together for both education and fellowship. These men understand the challenges you will face in the ministry unlike anyone else and can be a tremendous resource for support and perspective when issues present themselves. We are to be a synergistic team working for the advancement of the Kingdom of God. Always remember, it is not a competition between pastors and their churches—there are always enough people in your community to fill your church and your brother's church as well.

William Mitchell does a great job of explaining the importance of teamwork in his book, "Winning in the Land of the Giants:" "We don't play the game of life on our own, although we may think we do. We can't do what we do without the help of a great many other people, some seen and some unseen. We are on a team whether we want to be or not. And as team members, we have obligations to the team." [57]

The Apostle Paul admonished young Timothy in II Timothy 2:2 when he said, "'And what you have heard from me in the presence of many witnesses, commit to faithful men who will be able to teach others also.'" Even though Timothy was a young man, he was encouraged to pass on those things which had been committed to other faithful men so they could teach others. It was the transference of wisdom, one generation to the next. We, too, are responsible for mentoring and passing on what God has taught us throughout our lives—from our generational experiences to upcoming pastors. If we start passing on our experiences at an early age, it will become second nature by the time we are well advanced in years and we will have helped countless numbers of others along the way. In doing this, you will be bringing the next generation alongside of you as you grow and mature in your ministry and you will be modeling what they are to do for those who come after them.

I preached my first sermon 65 years ago though it seems like it's just been few years. Too soon, our lives are spent and we've missed the opportunity to pass on the great truths and lessons we've received from the Lord to those who come after us. Don't wait until you feel prepared to share and mentor and model. Do it now! Build strong relationships that will endure and strengthen others so that they may carry on when you're gone.

2 Cherish and Protect Friendships

I feel very fortunate that God has given me a disposition that makes it easy for me to relate to others. I love being with people and I love people! Throughout my ministry, God has given me many opportunities to encourage others and to build strong relationships along the way. Carol Ann and I have always had a great many we consider as friends, but very few we count as *close* friends. I've heard it said that if you have five friends in your life you could count on to stand by you regardless the challenge, you are, indeed, very fortunate. I am blessed to have many more than just five friends I could call on at any time, whatever the need, but these deep, deep friendships have been a long time in the making. You have to go through lots of experiences over many years to develop friendships such as these.

In your role as a pastor, you must value and protect these friendships fiercely. Friendships of great depth must develop naturally and can't be contrived or coerced. You have to travel through lots of experiences—both good and bad—to be sure your friendships are truly trustworthy. One way I've found to be a sort of litmus test of friendship is to ask myself, "Is this friend someone I could tell of a moral or ethical failure on my part and be sure it would go no further?" This one question—if answered truthfully—thins the list of trustworthy friends pretty fast!

Friendships developed over the course of a lifetime will eventually reach a point wherein anything can be discussed without threatening the bond. This is true even if you don't see one another very often, but when you do reunite, it is as if no time has passed and you pick up right where you left off. If you are blessed with friendships such as these, cherish and protect them with your life.

I can tell you such friends as this are literally lifesavers. In one particularly dark period of my life, I called such a friend to share my heartache. Without me so much as asking, he immediately got on a plane and flew to where we were living and stayed for three days. He just knew I needed him at that time. His faithfulness during those short days made the difference between moving through that time in victory or despair and I'll never forget it.

Every pastor needs a friend like that. Maybe more than one. Pray for this throughout your ministry and realize when your friendships do develop, they are God's gift to you. Do what it takes to contribute to and strengthen these relationships because you never know when you will need that lifetime friend.

2 Keep Confidences

It should go without saying, but it is of *extreme* importance to not reveal anything someone has told you in confidence. Let those who share with you in confidence have the peace of mind to know that whatever they say, you will not repeat it. Be especially vigilant not to use stories shared as sermon illustrations, regardless if you have changed the names, the setting, and even some of the particulars. Nothing will destroy your integrity and credibility within your church more quickly than for you to betray the confidences people have shared with you.

It is especially important not to share the confidences of other pastors, even under the covering of asking for prayer. I know of one pastor who was struggling with internet pornography and asked two pastor friends to pray for him and his struggles. These men, in turn, shared their friend's struggles with a few of their deacons asking for their prayers as well. It wasn't long before the news reached the lay leaders of the troubled pastor's church where he was quickly fired. This man asked for prayer and the support of faithful friends, but what he received was shame and dishonor and the loss of his life's work—all because his friends broke his confidence.

I have personal experience where I learned the all-too-hurtful consequence of breaking a confidence while asking for prayer. I was meeting with staff members at a church when one of the leaders confided in me a deeply personal problem she had developed with one of her children. She asked me not to share any of the details with anyone. I wasn't thinking clearly when I shared her story with her staff leader, again, asking for prayer for her and her family.

Innocently enough, the staff leader later mentioned to the woman he had been praying for her and mentioned the issue she had shared with me in private. I sincerely meant well because I concluded that her supervisor should know of the circumstances, but I was wrong in my presumption. This one transgression forever ruptured our relationship and she never confided in me again. She was right not to do so because I had betrayed her confidence.

Something like that never happened again and I'll never forget the impression it made on me to keep in confidence what is meant to be kept in confidence. If those who confide in you want others to know, let it be come from them, on their terms. Your job is to pray, offer guidance, and provide encouragement without repeating anything.

2

Lead by Example

You cannot lead people to do what you will not do yourself. You must be willing to get in the trenches and work alongside your staff, lay leaders, and church members. Your actions and words set the tone for the engagement of all you influence. You are the bar against which others will measure their involvement so you must act accordingly. Though it is a lot of responsibility to shoulder, your people expect you to lead. That's also the opinion of W. W. Melton in "The Making of a Preacher:" "Seldom does a church go beyond the leadership of the pastor. They wait for him to blaze the trail before they go forward." [58] The 'do as I say, not as I do' practice has never worked when leading people and never will. People will follow you if you lead the way in your own life and actions.

If you want to have a soul-winning church, you have to be a soul-winner. If you want to have a generous church, you need to be generous in every way. If you are pursuing debt-free operations for the church, you need to practice the same financial principles in your own life. This is an especially important principle for individuals and the church.

Show your people that you are a lifelong learner, that your thirst for learning more about Christ is endless. In "Leading Change," John Kotter makes a solid case for continual learning: "Lifelong learners actively solicit opinions and ideas from others. They don't make the assumption that they know it all or that most other people have little to contribute. Just the opposite, they believe that with the right approach, they can learn from anyone under almost any circumstance." [59] Kotter has a valid point—you are never through learning and gaining new insights into ministry. Strive to have a teachable spirit and work to continually develop your skills.

Because the ministry is one of the few vocations that doesn't require continuing education, recertification, or skills renewal, it is incumbent upon you to take the initiative to do it for you, your church, and to best honor God. There are frequently ministerial meetings, regional or national conferences, and virtually unlimited resources and references online. With such resources available, there is really no reason why all of us cannot increase our ministry abilities and deepen our understanding of Christian truth, strengthen our leadership skills, and further refine and define our Biblical worldview, cultural awareness, and principles for working well with others.

When we keep our hearts turned toward the Lord and our minds filled with every bit of knowledge that we can soak up, we will be at our most effective in service to the church. In doing so, you will set the example as to how a minister should function and lead and serve as an desirable example for others to follow.

2

When You're Wrong, Admit It

It is important that you be willing to say, "I was wrong; please forgive me. It won't happen again." Whether you're addressing your deacon body, your congregation, or your fellow pastors, sometimes things just don't go according to our plan. When that happens, take the initiative to offer your apology before you're asked to. Ask forgiveness and commit to never letting the same mistake happen again. In doing so, you are humbling yourself before those most closely affected and making a promise to do your best to never allow it to happen again. Genuine humility has a great impact on others, regardless of the fall-out from the mistake.

When I was pastor at First Southern Baptist Church of Del City, Oklahoma, I remember very vividly the words of my deacons. They said, "Pastor, we will follow you anywhere once, but don't make the same mistake twice!" They meant they were behind me all the way, but not to test their resolve if I didn't learn from my mistakes. I made my share of errors while I was there, but was always ready with a sincere apology and the promise not to repeat the mistake.

One year while at this church I had what I thought was a great idea for a special family night at the Music Hall in downtown Oklahoma City. Pat Boone was still attracting large crowds, especially within the Christian community, and I thought it would be a great opportunity for our church to sponsor such a wholesome, family-oriented show. Pat did come and put on a wonderful show. Our people loved him and his strong Christian stand made him a favorite. The glitch of the evening came when I realized it was also opening night of the Oklahoma State Fair—a huge event that drew thousands—especially on the first day!

We had a nice crowd come to our show, but not near what we had hoped for when we were originally planning the event. And it all came down to me and my lack of doing sufficient research to realize such a huge event was already scheduled. As soon as possible, I met with the deacons and assumed full responsibility for the ill planning. I told them, "This was a mistake and I apologize. It won't ever happen again." That was really all they needed to hear from me. They knew it was a mistake on my part and my admission only strengthened their confidence in me and my leadership.

"I was wrong."

"I'm sorry."

"Please forgive me."

"It won't happen again."

These are all important phrases for a pastor to use whenever necessary. Believe me, I have had to apologize on more than one occasion for words and actions that were inappropriate in either their spirit or content. I have found that most people will readily accept such an acknowledgement when it is genuinely and freely given. I have had to do this more times than I would like to admit, but there are just times in our lives when we make mistakes. The best thing we can do is to accept it and admit it to others. People will appreciate you for acknowledging it and come to respect you for it, too.

2 Be a Grateful Person

The Bible tells us time and again to have a grateful heart. It doesn't say when everything is going well or you feel like, but to have a grateful heart always. Here are just a few verses that present the importance of being grateful:

"Give thanks to the Lord, for He is good;
His faithful love endures forever…
Let them offer sacrifices of thanksgiving and announce His works with shouts of joy."

–Psalms 107:1, 22

"I will offer You a sacrifice of thanksgiving and call on the name of Yahweh." –Psalm 116:17

"…I will sacrifice to You with a voice of thanksgiving…" –Jonah 2:9

"Let us enter His presence with thanksgiving;
Let us shout triumphantly to Him in song"

–Psalm 95:2

"Enter His gates with thanksgiving and His courts with praise. Give thanks to Him and praise His name." –Psalm 100:4

"When you sacrifice a thank offering to the Lord, sacrifice it so that you may be accepted."

–Leviticus 22:29

I love what Joseph Stowell says in "Reclaiming a Passion for What Endures: Eternity" about being grateful: "Kingdom people live with an unconquerable sense of gratitude. Paul states that in light of our deliverance, we are to give thanks to the Father who made our citizenship in the eternal kingdom possible." [60] Isn't that a great description? Unconquerable sense of gratitude.

Jesus' experience with the 10 lepers shows just how much He valued gratitude. He wasn't asking for anything undue—just a simple acknowledgement for all he had done for them. The return on His investment, however, was anything but gracious. Here's the story from Luke 17:

"While traveling to Jerusalem, He passed between Samaria and Galilee. As He entered a village, 10 men with serious skin diseases met Him. They stood at a distance and raised their voices, saying, 'Jesus, Master, have mercy on us!' When He saw them, He told them, 'Go and show yourselves to the priests.' And while they were going, they were healed.

But one of them, seeing that he was healed, returned and, with a loud voice, gave glory to God. He fell facedown at His feet, thanking Him. And he was a Samaritan.

The Jesus said, 'Were not 10 cleansed? Where are the other nine? Didn't any return to give glory to God except this foreigner?' –Luke 17:11-18

Paul learned the hard way the importance of showing gratitude after his visits to Philippi proved to be painful and disappointing to him. While there, he was falsely accused, arrested, beaten, put in stocks in the inner dungeon, and even lived through an earthquake while being imprisoned. But he was not to be discouraged from his call to serve. Hear the conviction of his words in Philippians: "'I give thanks to my God for every remembrance of you,...'" (Philippians 1:3). He is thanking God for every encounter he had with them despite the hostility they first showed toward him. Paul's perspective here is valuable for us: Remember the best and forget the rest! In doing so, you will nurture and develop a grateful attitude.

Paul continued speaking to the Philippians, this time stressing the need for Christ in all situations. His challenge to them is one of the most oft-quoted verses in the Bible, and for a very good reason—he speaks firsthand about the truth of a relationship with Jesus. This is his encouragement to the Philippians:

"Rejoice in the Lord always. I will say it again:
Rejoice! Let your graciousness be known to

everyone. The Lord is near. Don't worry about anything; but in everything, through prayer and petition with thanksgiving, let your requests be made known to God. And the peace of God, which surpasses every thought, will guard your hearts and minds in Christ Jesus."

–Philippians 4:4-7

To the Ephesians, he urged them to give thanks: "...for everything to God the Father in the name of our Lord Jesus Christ..." –Ephesians 5:20

To the Corinthians he wrote:
"Now the One who provides seed for the sower and bread for food will provide and multiply your seed and increase the harvest of your righteousness. You will be enriched in every way for all generosity, which produces thanksgiving to God through us. For the ministry of this service is not only supplying the needs of the saints, but is also overflowing in many acts of thanksgiving to God." –II Corinthians 9:10-12

And lastly, to the Colossians:
"Devote yourselves to prayer; stay alert in it with thanksgiving." –Colossians 4:2

These challenges by Paul as well as many others throughout Scripture make it clear: we are to be filled with gratitude for everything God allows into our lives.

My mother had polio from the time she was 10 months old. Her early years were marked by one surgery after another, numbering more than a dozen by the time she was 15. It was such an ordinary part of her life, that many times she rode the train from Little Rock to St. Louis by herself to have surgery. The doctors did all they could, but ultimately one leg remained 6" shorter than the other and one foot was several sizes smaller than the other. All of her life she was crippled and was never able to do most of the normal activities of childhood.

When my father died at age 52 and left her widowed, she came to live with us and did so for the next 30 years. Her final two years were spent in an assisted living facility because we were unable to care for her adequately. And yet, despite all of the misfortunes of her life, she was the happiest person I've even known.

All of my years growing up were filled with efforts to help her do whatever she needed done. She never once took my help for granted and thanked me every time I did something for her. As she got older, she never lost her grateful outlook as some people do. When my cousin asked her, "Aunt Lois, if you have to go into a rest home, how will you feel about that?" Mother was quick to reply, "Well, I won't want to do it, but if I do, I will be the happiest person there!" And you know what? She was!

Just a few months before her death, she told me, "I am really happy here," and I knew she meant it. She demonstrated for me, my family, and so many others, that happiness is a choice and gratitude is the source of a happy life.

William Mitchell makes a great point concerning the importance of attitudes when he says, "Attitudes are more important than facts. They are controlling valves for our behavior. We think in a certain way over time...Attitudes also produce behavior of a like kind. Positive attitudes result in positive behavior." [61] For me, the attitude of gratitude is a great source of strength in my life.

Don't Be Disloyal

Beyond a personal faith in Christ, the number one quality I look for in coworkers is loyalty. This is a character trait that must be developed, tested, and strengthened. You cannot buy loyalty. There's really not a lot a gray area when it comes to matters of loyalty—a person is either loyal or they are not. The effects of a disloyal person in your ranks will destroy your effectiveness as a leader. No matter your issues with someone, especially staff members, you should never speak negatively about them in public. To do so undermines your ministry and destroys the confidence of others within the church.

When I served as Associate Pastor of First Baptist Church Dallas, I led the staff and general ministries of the church. To this day, I still say some of the greatest people

I have ever worked with were on that staff. At one point in my tenure there I began to encounter criticisms and regular opposition from several of the staff members. I tried every approach I could think of to address the disloyalty from the vocal few including substantial increases in salary during my first 18 months on the job.

I served them with energy and kindness. I worked in every way I could think of to help them succeed in their ministries. I always treated them with respect and made it a point to express my appreciation for their tireless work and increased their compensation significantly. And then I learned a valuable lesson: You can't pay someone enough to be loyal. Either they are loyal or they are not. A disloyal person can cause far-reaching problems in your ministry and can never be considered a positive contributor to the health and success of your organization.

As far as I'm concerned, disloyalty is a fatal character flaw because it shows you as one who cannot be trusted. Disloyal people always find themselves embroiled in turmoil and transition, moving from or causing dissent wherever they land. That said, I firmly believe that the best remedy for this unsavory behavior is to repay it with, you guessed it, more loyalty. Be the example Christ set whether your team members are or not.

Don't Take Criticism Personally and *Don't Believe All the Praise You Get Either*

2

You've probably heard of people who have fallen into the trap of believing their own press clippings—all flattery and no substance. The result is that they think they're infallible, much greater than they really are. It works the same with criticisms and critiques, too, in reverse. You can't believe everything you hear or read about yourself—positive or negative. If you do, your effectiveness will suffer greatly.

Simply put, none of us deserve to be saved or used in the ministry. Whatever good comes out of us is from the Lord. Therefore, no credit is due us; we're simply the vessels the Lord is using to accomplish His means. If we can begin to grasp our unworthiness and understand the miracle of our salvation and call to ministry, then neither praise nor criticism will affect us.

Jesus warned the religious leaders of His time not to go out of their way to elicit praise from others. He told them all such praise was of no use and utterly worthless. This is His challenge from the Sermon on the Mount:

> "Be careful not to practice your righteousness in front of people, to be seen by them. Otherwise, you will have no reward from your Father in heaven. So whenever you give to the poor, don't sound a trumpet before you, as the hypocrites

do in the synagogues and on the streets, to be applauded by people. I assure you: They've got their reward! But when you give to the poor, don't let your left hand know what your right hand is doing, so that your giving may be in secret. And your Father who sees in secret will reward you."

–Matthew 6:1-4

And then He continues:

"Whenever you fast, don't be sad-faced like the hypocrites. For they make their faces unattractive so their fasting is obvious to people. I assure you: They've got their reward!" –Matthew 6:16

Paul counseled the people of Corinth to keep this perspective when considering their self-worth apart from God:

"Brothers, consider your calling: Not many are wise from a human perspective, not many powerful, not many of noble birth. Instead, God has chosen what is foolish in the world to shame the wise, and God has chosen what is weak in the world to shame the strong. God has chosen what is insignificant and despised in the world—what is viewed as nothing—to bring to nothing what is viewed as something, so that no one can boast in His presence. But it is from Him that you are in Christ Jesus, who became God-given wisdom for us—our righteousness, sanctification, and redemption, in order that, as it is written: The one who boasts must boast in the Lord."

—I Corinthians 1:26-30

In his second letter to the people of Corinth, he put it this way:

"Now we have this treasure in clay jars, so that this extraordinary power may be from God and not from us." —II Corinthians 4:7

Peter had similar words when addressing the Christians scattered across the Roman Empire:

"Therefore, as a fellow elder and witness to the sufferings of the Messiah and also a participant in the glory about to be revealed, I exhort the elders among you; Shepherd God's flock among you, not overseeing out of compulsion but freely, according to God's will; not for the money but eagerly; not lording it over those entrusted to you, but being examples to the flock. And when the chief Shepherd appears, you will receive the unfading crown of glory." —I Peter 5:1-4

Don't ever think so highly of yourself that you leave God out of the picture. God uses all of us in spite of us, not because of us. We are the most privileged people in all the world to have any part in God's Kingdom. To be saved is a remarkable miracle as is the opportunity to serve the Lord and minister in His name. While it is nice to receive praise, it can easily divert our attention from the Lord to ourselves and lead us to self-dependency rather than God-dependency.

The counter to praise is criticism and is rarely nice to receive. It can be hard to take or to be questioned about how and why we do certain things or hold such beliefs. Find comfort in knowing that Jesus was criticized harshly and often throughout His ministry on earth. You have to work at it not to allow criticism to detour you from the calling God has placed on your life.

Before you react to criticism, determine if it is valid or not. If it is valid, you need to develop a strategy to correct it. If it is not, make every effort to respond with care. Ask yourself

- Is the person who made the criticism a devoted individual whose judgment is sought after by others?

- Is the person fully committed to the church and a positive influence in the fellowship?

- Is the person one who often creates havoc in the church?

In asking these questions and others that come to mind, you will best be able to determine how to react to the criticism. If it is constructive, determine to react in a positive way; if it is negative, your response should still be kind and thoughtful. I strongly urge you to always have a third party present whenever you are confronting a specific criticism about something you have done or some aspect of your ministry. This is for the protection of all parties involved. The bottom line regarding criticism is this: sometimes it is helpful, sometimes it is hurtful, but at all times respond with kindness and respect. It is what Jesus did and what He asks of us.

Learn to Listen...Or You'll Never Learn!

2

You've probably heard the reason we have two ears and only one mouth–it's because we should listen twice as much as we speak. When you talk incessantly, it reveals your insecurities—about yourself, your subject matter, or your position. Confident people say what they need to and allow it to stand on its own merit. Make it a point not to dominate every discussion and to value the input of others. In doing so, you will learn far more than you ever would if you were doing all the talking!

Surround yourself with people who will tell you the truth, not just what they think you want to hear. Listen to your congregation and it leaders. If they thought enough of an issue to share it with you, rest assured, it's important to them. They can bring a perspective or opinion that you might not otherwise have considered. After all, you're not the only one in the room with keen powers of observation and wise decision-making skills.

Ironically, being able to hear the bad news can be the good news. That's because, if you never hear the negative or bothersome issues affecting your people, you can never correct them. It's a great illustration of what my mom used to always tell me: "Son, you aren't learning anything when you're the one doing the talking!" If you aren't receptive to the cares and concerns of your members, you will build up obstacles of communication that can become difficult to overcome. The result is your communication becomes one-sided and obsolete; yours is the only opinion that matters and the only one considered worthy. If you aren't open to the 'bad news,' you'll never receive the 'good news' either.

Many of your members just want to be heard, to know that their voice counts for something. Many of them may end up feeling as if no one cares what they think and leadership is too busy to be concerned. This is especially important regarding controversial issues or deep spiritual discussions. We all need to be sensitive at these times and not just give out easy answers when people start to ask questions. As ministry leaders, we need to take the time to listen to them and allow them the opportunity to 'have their say.' In the end, your willingness to hear them out and address their questions and concern will make for members who feel valued and appreciated.

In one church where I served as pastor, there was a man who voted against everything. In fact, I'm pretty sure he felt it was 'his calling' to give a negative vote every time. He told me,

"I voted against you when you came in view of a call to our church. I was not against you, but I thought if one vote would make you not come, then you probably should not be our pastor." We ended up becoming best friends. He eventually took me on one of the real adventures of my life—canoeing down the Illinois River in February! And yes, it was freezing!

The lesson here is that we became friends because I listened to him. The night we voted to build our new auditorium, we presented a recommendation that we shorten the auditorium by 25 feet and eliminate close to 500 seats. Not surprisingly, he voted against the recommendation. When he stood to speak against the motion, I asked him to come to the platform and use the microphone so everyone could hear his concerns. He did, but still the motion passed. This same process was repeated in nearly every business meeting that required a vote to accomplish something: he got his opportunity to speak and the people voted him down every time. He wasn't discouraged because he was voted down; he was happy because he was allowed to speak and be heard.

While you can't expect every negative opinion to be resolved like that, it is still imperative to listen to others before making any significant decision concerning the church. When you hear the words of others, it's a win-win situation—you gain a new insight (possibly one you had never considered before!) and the speaker is validated. And in the case of the auditorium…my friend who lobbied for the larger auditorium was right—we should have listened to him!

This excerpt from Christie Craig's August, 2012, blog shows the power in listening, even when all we want to do is jump in and speak!—

We all know what it's like to get that phone call in the middle of the night. This night's call was no different. Jerking up to the ringing summons, I focused on the red illuminated numbers of my clock. Midnight. Panicky thoughts filled my sleep-dazed mind as I grabbed the receiver.

"Hello?"

My heart pounded. I gripped the phone tighter and eyed my husband, who was now turning to face my side of the bed.

"Mama?"

I could hardly hear the whisper over the static. But my thoughts immediately went to my daughter. When the desperate sound of a young crying voice became clearer on the line, I grabbed for my husband and squeezed his wrist.

"Mama, I know it's late. But don't...don't say anything, until I finish. And before you ask, yes, I've been drinking. I nearly ran off the road a few miles back and..."

I drew in a sharp shallow breath, released my husband and pressed my hand against my forehead. Sleep still fogged my mind, and I attempted to fight back the panic. Something wasn't right.

"And I got so scared. All I could think about was how it would hurt you if a policeman came to your door and I'd been killed. I want...to come home. I know running away was wrong. I know you've been worried sick. I should have called you days ago, but I was afraid…"

Sobs of deep-felt emotion flowed from the receiver and poured into my heart. Immediately I pictured my daughter's face in my mind and my fogged senses seemed to clear. "I think—"

"No! Please let me finish! Please!"

She pleaded not so much in anger, but in desperation. I paused and tried to think what to say. Before I could go on, she continued.

"I'm pregnant, Mama. I know I shouldn't be drinking now…especially now, but I'm scared, Mama. So scared!"

The voice broke again, and I bit into my lip, feeling my own eyes fill with moisture. I looked at my husband who sat silently mouthing, "Who is it?"

I shook my head and when I didn't answer, he jumped up and left the room, returning seconds later with the portable phone held to his ear. She must have heard the click in the line because she continued, "Are you still there? Please don't hang up on me! I need you. I feel so alone."

I clutched the phone and stared at my husband, seeking guidance.

"I'm here, I wouldn't hang up," I said.

"I should have told you, Mama. I know I should have told you. But when we talk, you just keep telling me what I should do. You read all those pamphlets on how to talk about sex and all, but all you do is talk. You don't listen to me. You never let me tell you how I feel. It is as if my feelings aren't important. Because you're my mother you think you have all the answers. But sometimes I don't need answers. I just want someone to listen."

I swallowed the lump in my throat and stared at the how-to-talk-to-your-kids pamphlets scattered on my nightstand. "I'm listening," I whispered.

"You know, back there on the road, after I got the car under control, I started thinking about the baby and taking care of it. Then I saw this phone booth, and it was as if I could hear you preaching about how people shouldn't drink and drive. So I called a taxi. I want to come home."

"That's good, Honey," I said, relief filling my chest. My husband came closer, sat down beside me and laced his fingers through mine. I knew from his touch that he thought I was doing and saying the right thing.

"But you know, I think I can drive now."

"No!" I snapped. My muscles stiffened, and I tightened the clasp on my husband's hand. "Please, wait for the taxi. Don't hang up on me until the taxi gets there."

"I just want to come home, Mama."

"I know. But do this for your mama. Wait for the taxi, please."

I listened to the silence in fear. When I didn't hear her answer, I bit into my lip and closed my eyes. Somehow I had to stop her from driving.

"There's the taxi, now."

Only when I heard someone in the background asking about a Yellow Cab did I feel my tension easing.

"I'm coming home, Mama."

There was a click and the phone went silent.

Moving from the bed, tears forming in my eyes, I walked out into the hall and went to stand in my sixteen-year-old daughter's room. The dark silence hung thick. My husband came from behind, wrapped his arms around me and rested his chin on the top of my head.

I wiped the tears from my cheeks. "We have to learn to listen," I said to him.

He pulled me around to face him. "We'll learn. You'll see." The he took me into his arms, and I buried my head in his shoulder.

I let him hold me for several moments, then I pulled back and stared at the bed. He studied me for a second, then asked, "Do you think she'll ever know she dialed the wrong number?"

I looked at our sleeping daughter, then back at him. "Maybe it wasn't such a wrong number."

"Mom, Dad, what are you doing?" The muffled young voice came from under the covers.

I walked over to my daughter, who now sat up staring into the darkness. "We're practicing," I answered.

"Practicing what?" she mumbled and laid back on the mattress, her eyes already closed in slumber.

"Listening," I whispered and brushed a hand over her cheek. [62]

It's a powerful story, but makes the point soundly: Learn to listen or you won't learn at all!

2 You Work With Others—They Don't Work For You!

There is a big difference between working for someone and working with someone. And the difference is astounding! It is the difference between perpetuating an autocracy or building a team. As church leaders, we must be the kind of leaders who can lead in building an effective team for ministry.

There are no unimportant people in God's economy. Each of us is made in the image of God and each of us has eternal significance in God's redemptive purposes. God has a plan for every one of our lives. David declared God's grand design for each of us in Psalms: "Your eyes saw me when I was formless; all my days were written in Your book and planned before a single one of them began" (Psalm 139:16).

Let that soak in for a bit. It's almost unfathomable, but true. God saw you as a person before your body ever began to take form. Before you were ever conceived, God saw you. What an incredible truth! Just think about all the billions of people that have lived since the creation of the world...and God saw each of them before their form ever took shape.

It is without question that God has a plan for every one of our lives. And so it follows that every individual is absolutely precious to our God. If God so views each one of us like that, then how can any of us even entertain the thought that we are superior to others? We all have different roles, uniquely designed to best suit our particular God-given gifts and abilities for service in the Kingdom. As a Christian leader, you will minister to others who also have an assignment from God. And even though it may differ from yours greatly, you must give them the courtesy, kindness, and respect their place in God's Kingdom demands. Lift them up whenever possible and look for ways to bring out the best in them. They work with you, so help them to succeed. They are not your competitors, but bring complementary gifts and talents that God has place within them to work alongside you.

Lead in love and be careful not to give commands as if to imply obedience to you is their only task. Pour your life into them; serve them; assist them. Be sensitive to your team's needs and work to build trust and confidence with them. As a commander-in-chief, you will only receive their skills; as their servant-leader, you will receive their heart's best efforts. When you see yourself as a partner in ministry with others, God will anoint your efforts together.

While at LifeWay, I once had a strong leader on our staff who was one of the most talented individuals I had ever met. His credentials were exceptional. He had great training at one of the most prestigious universities in America. He understood business well and was creative in his leadership style. The one thing he did not have, however, was the attitude of a team player. Everywhere he went, he sowed seeds of discord and dissension. He defied the trustees and disrupted the effectiveness of our entire leadership team. Ultimately, I had to remove him from his position because his attitude and actions created havoc. He is not alive today, but he still remains as one of the biggest challenges I've ever faced in my ministry.

I caution you to beware of anyone who is not supportive of the entire organization. Your staff will have differences of opinion, but they must be fully on board with the mission of your ministry. No matter your assignment within a church, remember we all work together towards the same goal. No one is more important than the team on which he works.

2 Don't Be Threatened if People Love Their Former Minister

One of the challenges in ministry that you will almost inevitably face is how to relate to your predecessor in your position. My dad always told me that if they loved their former pastor, it means they have the capacity to love me. That was of great comfort as I followed several greatly loved pastors.

Don't be threatened by the memories and methods of your predecessor. If possible, get to know him and develop a relationship. He can offer insights into your new position that no one else would have. If he is still involved in ministry, invite him back to the church to preach or to speak and to honor him for his service to the church. This can help diminish most, if not all, of the resistance you might experience in the early days at your new church. Your members will appreciate you showing kindness and respect to someone they have known and loved for years.

As the Book of Joshua begins, God tells Joshua what he must do next:

> "'Moses My servant is dead. Now you and all the people prepare to cross over the Jordan to the land I am giving the Israelites.'" –Joshua 1:2

At first, it almost seems as if the Lord is abruptly moving on from all Moses had done for His people and focused solely on Joshua. But that is far from the case. Moses led the Israelites away from Egyptian bondage and through the wilderness for 40 years and would always be regarded as one of Israel's greatest leaders. In fact, he is mentioned 81 times in the New Testament and Joshua is only recognized three times. Moses would not be forgotten; but the time had come to move on and to take possession of The Promised Land.

However much your staff and members may have loved your predecessor, when you arrive, it is time to begin the transition process and move on. Respect and honor him, but help the people understand that the real legacy of any leader is what happens after he leaves, not while he is still present in the role. Your people will learn to love and appreciate you if you show kindness, appreciation, and respect for those who came before you.

2 Face Problems Head-On and Deal with Them Quickly

As soon as you know of a significant problem developing in the church, address it and work to resolve it. The sooner you address an issue, the less chance it has to gain any momentum and become unnecessarily overblown. Don't allow the discord to fester and don't avoid the confrontation by living with ambiguity.

Most church conflicts involve staff members or key leaders within the church. Expect and plan for such disappointments among these relationships and establish a principle and strategy for such times. Determine in advance that you will give everyone the benefit of the doubt and that errors or miscommunications were not done intentionally. Build your relationships upon the belief that your team would not deliberately hurt you or impair your leadership efforts. When the occasion arises that it seems they have done something specifically inappropriate, go to them and let them know that you don't want to believe they would do so. If they admit to having done it, deal with it immediately and without hesitation. And always with kindness!

If severe enough, the situation may require termination of the individual from their responsibilities. Always involve the appropriate committee in the church or leaders in the institution in that decision. This is always a difficult time for you *and* them. If it needs to be done, however, do it with grace. Never enter into a termination situation by yourself; always have another individual present with you. Resist the challenge to get into a situation where it is your word against another's. The third party can verify the accuracy of whatever must be said about the individual.

Again, let graciousness, kindness, and respect be your guides in dealing with these situations. I have had to dismiss two staff members during my 35 years as a pastor and three close associates in my 15 years at LifeWay. None of these individuals were happy about it, but none of them were able to complain about how they were treated in the termination process.

Smaller conflicts also need immediate attention. They also need to be dealt with in love and kindness. Don't allow dissention and division to feed off the conflict. When you resolve, in advance, to address conflicts in the spirit of Christ, dealing with them as unto the Lord, and treating each other with grace, you can know you've done your best. When conflicts cannot ultimately be resolved without a termination or a resignation, let it happen, but do so with a tear and not a shout of rejoicing.

My very first pastorate was in a small community just outside Bryan/College Station, TX. It was a wonderful church, filled with some of the greatest people I have ever known. To this day, some 60 years later, I still have relationships with some of them! I learned a very valuable lesson in dealing with conflict from these people.

One day, one of our church members and Sunday School teacher, George Cargill, came to me and said that a fellow member, Esker Martin, was angry with him but he didn't know why. Esker was in George's class, but had recently quit speaking to him. Those were all the details I had.

I was just 20 years old and new at being a pastor, so I handled it the best way I knew how—I went directly to Esker's house and found him out in his cornfield. When I asked him why he wasn't speaking to George, he explained that his grandson had just been put in prison and that the Sunday School lesson that day was about ministering to those in prison. He thought George had deliberately taught that lesson to insult him and his family.

What he didn't realize is that the lesson was the one the Sunday School Board had prepared well in advance and put into the quarterly to teach that Sunday. George had no idea about his grandson. When I asked him if he would tell George what he told me, he agreed.

I went to the home of the chairman of our deacons and asked him to come with me. We picked up George and headed back to Esker's tiny white frame farmhouse. In Esker's very small living room, the four of us convened, one on each side of the room. Then, I asked Esker to explain why he had quit speaking to George. When he was finished, George quickly apologized, asked forgiveness, and explained that he didn't know anything of Esker's grandson's imprisonment. Then Esker forgave George for the misunderstanding and I witnessed one of the most blessed moments of my ministry— seeing two old saints embracing each other with tears of forgiveness and gratitude.

Since then, I've faced issues big and small and come to realize that every challenge has to be evaluated on its own. You have to determine what is important to deal with and what is not. Frequently, it is the difference between what is urgent and what is important, but not always so. Not every issue that is urgent is important. Conversely, not every issue that is important is urgent. Don't let someone else make *their* emergency *your* emergency! Ask these questions before you take immediate action:

- Is this issue detrimental to the life of the church?
- Is it something that can be worked out with careful communication and personal intervention?
- Is it something that requires action by the church?
- Who is the best person to address this issue?
- Does it involve the staff or personnel of the church?
- Is it a family matter and just needs some godly counseling or is it a matter of theological concern or threatening the fellowship and health of the church?

It is also helpful to remember that not everything can be confronted and settled at once. Sometimes it takes a series of actions and/or conversations over a span of time. Matthew 18 gives us an excellent pattern for dealing with problems in the church that create offenses between individuals. First, if the offense is against you, go to your brother and confront him privately. If he responds positively, you've won your brother over (Matthew 18:15). If not, then take one or two others with you so that the issue can be discussed thoroughly and facts confirmed (Matthew 18:16). If this also fails to bring about reconciliation, bring the matter before the church for consideration. Finally, if no accord is reached, then consider him as an outside and unbeliever (Matthew 18:17). This is the very last resort and not one you want to approach if at all avoidable. When you follow the instructions of Jesus, many conflicts can be resolved well before this point.

Jesus said,

"'Again, I assure you: If two of you on earth agree about any matter that you pray for, it will be done for you by My Father in heaven. For where two or three are gathered together in My name, I am there among them.'" –Matthew 18:19-20

These are the verses that immediately follow Jesus' instructions about how to deal with conflict. These are step-by-step directions *from* God *for* us in dealing with conflicts, misunderstandings, and offenses within the church. Whenever faced with these situations, ask the right questions, approach it as Jesus instructed us to, and trust God for the outcome. When you follow this plan, there are only two possible outcomes—reconciliation or discipline.

Problems never get better by themselves. When left unattended, they always grow beyond whatever the original issue was and complicate resolution. Always deal with problems directly, quickly, and with compassion. You can never drift anywhere worth going and problems are a prime example. Follow the Lord's instructions in this matter and God will bless.

Responsibility Without Accountability is Dangerous

2

I made it a practice as a pastor to meet with my deacon officers every Wednesday at 6:30 a.m. for a time of fellowship, prayer, and discussion. They knew these were times when they could ask me about anything or express any concerns. My relationships with these men grew stronger each week because of our shared time of fellowship, our partnership in ministry, our deepened friendships, and the accountability I maintained with them.

Those of us who lead or aspire to lead in the church must declare the Word of God with the ultimate authority it is. We must also remember that we are under its authority and are called to 'tremble' at God's Word. We must feel its authority upon our own lives as we allow it to affect everything we do.

The Scripture is inerrant, but I most certainly, am not! I must constantly guard against the mindset that allows me to preach to others and yet fail to heed the truth of the Scripture in my own life. I need to regularly seek counsel, insight, and the accountability of others to be my best. This is what Paul was referring to in I Corinthians 9:27 when he said, "Instead, I discipline my body and bring it under strict control, so that after preaching to others, I myself will not be disqualified.'" We don't have to commit some blatant sin or compromise of ethics to become disqualified. All we have to do is live as if we are above the message we preach to others. That's why maintaining some system of accountability is so important.

When I became president of LifeWay, the trustees had already established a Presidential Performance Review Committee which was set up to meet with the president regularly to assess his performance. Initially, they suggested doing away with the committee because of their trust in me. While flattered, I insisted that they keep the committee because I realized the danger in authority without accountability. I told them I did not want to fail for lack of supervision. Over the 15 years I served there, I met with that committee annually for evaluation, strategy projection, and vision casting for the organization.

Every pastor needs some form of accountability. It may be through regular meetings with deacon officers or other groups, but it is vital to effective ministry. Don't allow yourself to serve in a leadership position without the protection of supervision.

Pay Attention! Remember Names!

2

Early in my life I learned that the favorite word for each of us is our name. Whether we realize it or not, we all enjoy it when others remember our name. If you really want to impress someone, remember their name!

Just recently as we visited a church where I had served as interim pastor just a few years before. A young couple that was very active in the church while I was there came up to greet me and remind me of their first names. I nodded and then told them their last name! I doubt that they will ever forget that, after four years, their interim pastor remembered their names.

Many ministers I meet tell me they're just not good at remembering names, but I contend that it is something we can all do well. It all comes down to paying attention. For most of us, we are preoccupied when we first meet someone and oftentimes don't even hear their name correctly. If you pay attention from the start, you'll increase your chances of remembering them. Look them in the eye when meeting them and repeat their name back to them to make sure you understand them correctly. And, make an effort to use their name several times during that first conversation. This will help you recall them in future encounters.

When I was a senior in high school, a group of us founded the Christian Student Union at our school. Even 60+ years ago, it wasn't easy to start a new, Christian organization. The principal told us we needed 1,000 signatures of interested students before he would consider it. Our plan was to meet twice a week in the auditorium before classes began.

When we presented the signatures, he agreed to let us meet and we did so every Tuesday and Thursday mornings before school started. We were all student-led, though we did have a faculty sponsor. In January, before our graduation, we held a Christian Student Union banquet and invited Dr. Bill Tanner, a local pastor, to speak. I had not met him previously and only enjoyed a few minutes visiting with him during the banquet.

Months later, as a freshman at Baylor University, Dr. Tanner was our chapel speaker. I met him coming down the steps of Waco Hall. Mind you, I had only met him for a few minutes over nine months before and yet he still called me by name.

That made an impression on me that I have never forgotten. He was one of my all-time favorite people because he remembered my name. Remembering someone's name is the best way for you to show you really care about them. When you remember others' names, you will open the door to incredible moments of ministry.

Let me share another moment from my own ministry about remembering names. I received a letter from a young man I had led to the Lord and baptized back in 1977. He did not write me until 2004, but it was worth the wait.

"In 1977, when I was 18 years old, you met me for the first time in Glorieta, N.M. at a college retreat. At that time, I was certainly a very lost and angry young man. There had been many tough things I had lived through at that time of which you had no knowledge. I had been dragged to that conference kicking and screaming by a couple of friends at school. One night, you spoke to me for an extended length of time and, with great patience and kindness, listened to me express why I didn't believe in the God you had described. When you learned I was from Ft. Worth at the time, you invited me to come to FBC Euless when I returned. For the next 6 months, I pondered the things you told me and never once went back to church anywhere. At the end of that time, in my 18-year-old wisdom, I decided to test God. I would go to FBC Euless and see if you were the same and whether you remembered me. I remember thinking to myself that you wouldn't even know who I was or recall talking with me. At the end of the service, I waited and stood behind you as you were talking to others. When you turned around you didn't even allow me to get any words out of my mouth before you called me by name, welcomed me, and asked how I was doing. That act on that night was the most significant single thing that any other person has ever done for me before or since and I felt compelled to say thank you for allowing God to use you at that time to minister to me. At that moment, I vividly remember thinking that there must be something to this God you were talking about if you cared enough to remember my name after one meeting 6 months earlier."

That young man has become one of the top school administrators in the fourth largest city in America! He is still serving the Lord actively through his church!

Pay attention! Remember names!

3

Dealing With Change

3 Don't Be Afraid to Change

Change is the natural progression of all of life. There always has been, will be, and should be change. When you realize and accept this, it makes it easier to be prepared when change comes your way. Change is the one constant that everyone agrees upon and yet resists anyway. It is inevitable and it is futile to disregard or ignore it.

Refusing to face the reality of change can be a major challenge to leadership. Many times, it is opposed by people comfortable with the old way of doing things who are not open to new methods and processes. When you encounter resistance to change, be honest about what is happening and tell people what to expect along the way. Also, be flexible with the process—some things can be planned for when implementing change; others cannot.

While we cannot stop change, we can manage it and use it as a tool for progress. For each of us, all of our ways are in a constant state of transition. We're moving towards one goal or objective while moving away from another in our personal lives as well as ministry. This means that we must continually learn new skills, accept new opportunities, and always be focused on reinventing our ministries. Though our message never changes, how we communicate it must always adapt and change.

One of the best ways to facilitate a positive move towards change is to keep people's eyes focused on the future, not the past. When you give them information and inspiration, they can embrace a vision and a changed future. Going through change is not always a simple or easy process, but you must be willing to make changes to yourself and your ministry, or you will never change them for the better.

Personal transition and worldwide change are happening at warp speed now. Compared to just a generation ago, the change in personal communication has undergone a seismic shift. The changes of the last 30 years have been such that most things will never be the same again.

Take for example, the use of the internet. Back before we became a wired, global society, the widespread use of computers was unforeseeable. Consider this quote from Digital Equipment Corporation Chairman Ken Olson in 1987: "There is no reason anyone would want a computer in their home." [63]

These statistics show the transformation of digital communication and the impact personal computers and cell phones have had in less than 20 years:

- Today there are 280 million computers in homes in America or 87% of American homes; [64]
- There are over 2 billion people worldwide connected to the internet, sharing information at light speed on optic fiber and wireless networks. [65]
- Facebook was launched in 2004 and now has 1.3 billion users worldwide in 70 languages; 25% of users reside in the United States. Mobile phone users who

access Facebook on their mobile devices number approximately 680 million. Forty-eight percent of Facebook users log in daily to spend an average of 18 minutes per visit. There are 54,200,000 Facebook pages with 20,000,000 apps installed daily on them. The average Facebook user has what they consider to be 130 'friends.' Almost half of the users check Facebook when they wake up each day and more than a quarter check it before they even get out of bed! [66]

- YouTube is 10 years old and now has over 1 billion users. Incredibly, over 300 hours of video are uploaded every minute to the site. It is currently in 75 countries and in 61 languages. Eighty-two percent of teenagers, 14-17 years old, use YouTube. There are more than four billion views daily on the site. [67]

- Instagram was launched in 2010 and already has 78 million users in the United States, accounting for 28% of the population. [68]

- Twitter is less than a decade only but has been tremendously successful. Globally, there are 500 million tweets per day, accounting for the 300 billion tweets to date. Surprisingly, 77% of the Twitter accounts are outside of the United States and only 20% of regular internet users have Twitter accounts. However, worldwide there are more than 640 million Twitter accounts. Interestingly, the 55+ age demographic is the fastest growing segment of Twitter users. [69]

The refusal to believe that something truly new can happen is even more serious when it concerns our spiritual lives. When we are so close minded to believe that God cannot and will not do anything new, we are taking a backward look at our spiritual lives and run the risk of missing out on what He is already doing and what He is about to do.

If we're not open to change, we can see it as a threat—a threat to the way things have always been done, to our comfort level, and to having to try new and unknown things. One way to think of change is as a transition that catches us 'between' how things have been and how they are becoming.

Paul Tournier uses an illustration of a trapeze artist to show how important change can be: He reminds us that the trapeze artist glides out into the air, held only by a trapeze bar and that, at just the precise moment in his routine, he releases one bar and lunges for the one before him. He's done this thousands of times and knows the bar will be there for him yet, for one split-second, he hangs suspended in the air waiting to connect to the waiting bar. For what can seem like an eternity, an agonizing moment to be sure, the acrobat is mid-air with nothing to hold on to. He is literally between the bars.

That is the moment which most people fear in change. It is not so much where they have been or where they are going – the fear is that unknown in the middle, the actual time in between what was and what will be. This is much like the crisis created by change—the feeling that we are in between—not where we were, but not where we are yet going.

This is how it is frequently for us as believers and how we relate to change. On the one hand, we long for continuity and comfort, yet change is inevitable. We long for the eternal but must exist in the temporal. We deal with the transcendent while living in the immediate. It is a challenge we face throughout our physical and spiritual lives.

This tension, between the 'here and now' versus the future has a biblical description. When Paul wrote the church in Corinth, he wrote of being "in Christ" yet being "at Corinth" (I Corinthians 1:2). Even thousands of years ago, men experienced the tension of being between two worlds— the changelessness of Christ and chaos of living in Corinth.

Norman Pittenger described this tension between the balance we all seek—that of our personal identity in an ever-changing world—in his book, "The Historic Faith and a Changing World:" "It is indeed here that the balance in historic Christianity between the dogmas of the Incarnation and the Atonement is so valuable; for the assertion of Christian faith is that God not only saved man, through Christ from the confusions and contradictions of life in this world, but that He did it in this world and in the midst of those very confusions and contradictions. In a phrase, God made life safe at the center and meaningful at every point on the periphery." [70]

When life is safe and stable at the center, the speed of change on the outer edges makes no difference. It's much like the difference between an axle and a wheel. No matter how fast the wheel turns, the axle remains stable and unmoving.

When life is fixed at its center, the ever changing, faster moving outside circumstances still have no bearing on it. The hustle and bustle of life, no matter how hectic, will not change a fixed center. If we maintain the identity of Christ as the core of our life, we don't have to fear the changes of life. The church must trumpet the message that the identity at the center of life must remain constant even as change on the perimeter of life moves increasingly faster.

For all his wisdom, King Solomon couldn't have foreseen the digital revolution and the far-reaching impact it has had on how and why and when we do things. Though he was tremendously experienced and well versed in human nature and the news of his time, he was also jaded in his outlook concerning the future. As the author of Ecclesiastes, he went so far as to declare that nothing will ever be new again and there would be no further change in human history. Ever.

Undoubtedly the Bible is inerrant, but King Solomon's cynical forecast was not. These are his words concerning the future:

"What has been is what will be,

and what has been done is what will be done;

there is nothing new under the sun.

Can one say about anything,

"Look, this is new"?

It has already existed in the ages before us."

–Ecclesiastes 1:9-10

This is a fatalistic attitude that is prevalent in many churches—that things should not change because everything that should be present has already been with us for years. Concerning the unchanging Word of God, this is most definitely true, but concerning how to reach others with the Gospel, it is drastically off base.

The polar opposite to King Solomon's perspective has to be the Athenians that Paul describes on his visit to them. He said of them: "Now all the Athenians and the foreigners residing there spent their time on nothing else but telling or hearing something new" (Acts 17:21). These people were the internet surfers of their day. They would have been the first to be on Twitter, Facebook, Instagram, and YouTube. They lived for nothing other than to hear the latest and newest thing. They were more interested in the novelty of Paul's message than its actual content. Change was life for them and life was lived to enjoy change.

These two examples illustrate the biblical extremes of reaction to change. And as many things as have changed since these times, there still exists many people like each extreme. Some of us want everything like it was in our youth—the carefree lifestyle, a full life ahead of us, and opportunities around every corner. Contrarily, some of us reject anything the least bit dated as a relic and not relevant to the present. Neither extreme is a healthy attitude to have for your life or your ministry. The goal is to make changes as we move into the future, but carry with us those things which transcend time.

The prophet Isaiah shared another view of change that should characterize us all as believers. When speaking to the rebellious believers of Israel, this is what he said,

"This is what the Lord says - ...

'Do not remember the past events,

pay no attention to things of old.

Look, I am about to do something new;

even now it is coming. Do you not see it?

Indeed, I will make a way in the wilderness,

rivers in the desert.'"

–Isaiah 43:16, 18-19

The weary Israelites were hard-pressed on all sides. They had faced defeat by the Babylonians, seen the destruction of the City of David and the Temple of Solomon, and were facing what appeared to be the evident end of the great story that had begun with the call of Abraham and the eventual exodus of Moses. All around them loomed ruin, rubble, the end of their history, and only memories of what used to be. And then God said, "'I am about to do something new...'"

Two chapters later, the Lord clarifies His message: "'Remember what happened long ago, for I am God, and there is no other; I am God, and no one is like Me'" (Isaiah 46:9). This is just as relevant to us today in a world of cell phones and instant communication as it was before Christ walked the earth. Just as it was then, it is now: God wants us to know His nature and character never changes, but His works will continually change.

Demonstrate Courage, Don't Avoid Risk

Plato is credited with saying, "Courage is knowing what to fear." There's a lot of wisdom in just a few words. It doesn't tell us to be fearful or to be courageous; it just tells us how to tell the difference. Interestingly, the English word, 'crisis' is written in Chinese by combining two characters—one meaning 'danger,' and the other meaning 'opportunity.' That makes perfect sense, too—crises often arise when danger meets opportunity.

Dianna Booher explained courage well in her book, "The Esther Effect" when she said, "Courage is not the absence of fear. Courage comes in the face of fear. We unlearn fear by overcoming it, and we overcome fear by doing courageous things in the face of fear." [71]

I've heard it said, "Man cannot discover new oceans unless he has the courage to lose sight of the shore." This is true in so many aspects of our life. To be clear, however, courage is not doing foolish things and asking God to protect us or cause us to succeed. Christ-honoring courage must be accompanied by careful prayer, thought, and counsel. Our task is to submit our will to God's plan, His will, and His work and then to courageously follow it. In doing so, we will fulfill the charge of I Corinthians 10:31:

"Therefore, whether you eat or drink, or whatever you do, do everything for God's glory."

This is excellent counsel from David Dockery's "Christian Leadership Essentials:" "When we see the world as a broken place God wants to redeem, we need to have the convictions to tether us to the ancient and timeless Christian truths and to stir in us the courage to act as voices of redemption. Conviction without courage is hardly conviction." [72]

I remember reading an article by Paul Powell in the Texas Baptist Standard that said there were three kinds of pastors: caretakers, undertakers, and risk takers. In general, he is correct that most pastors fit neatly into one of these categories. The most dynamic of these is obviously, the risk taker—taking bigger chances, hoping for bigger returns. It is a calling that comes from the Lord and requires courage and wisdom that only God can give.

When I was pastor of First Southern Baptist Church in Del City, Oklahoma, we had a special Sunday afternoon and evening time at a local amusement park. It was a wonderful day of fun and fellowship. We concluded the day with a worship service at the park and had many people saved that day. We had never done anything like this before, so it took considerable courage on all our part, but God was in it through and through. In the end, we were blessed beyond measure!

Years later, while I was pastoring at First Baptist Church of Euless, we did a similar project. We stepped out in faith and held the first Christian Family Day ever at Six Flags Over

Texas. We rented the entire park on Friday before Easter. It was a big step of faith on our part because we had to sign a contract guaranteeing Six Flags $50,000 to secure the date. They explained how much we could charge and how much they would receive from each ticket sold. We had to sell 10,000 tickets just to break even.

On the day we reserved the park, we took over all the entertainment spots with Christian musicians and entertainers. We had continuous shows in the rodeo arena with one of the most popular groups around at the time. Each presentation had an evangelistic appeal. Our people manned the gates to let people in and we took care of everything within the park except for the rides and concession stands.

In return, we were free to witness and preach throughout the entire park. The first year we had over 14,000 people attend and God blessed it tremendously. We sponsored this same project for four years and saw our attendance numbers climb to 39,000 on the final one. Soon thereafter, Six Flags felt the event was firmly established and took it over as their own event, hosting Christian Family Day at most of their other parks as well. In the beginning, it was a risk that demanded courage from our people. But because God was in it, He honored our efforts and led us the entire way.

Once you know God is in a thing, build support with your members and don't hesitate to take action. It takes a great deal of courage to use every legitimate means available to you to reach the people with Gospel.

Elton Trueblood explains how we have become complacent in our zeal for sharing the Gospel compared to the early days of the Church. In "Alternative to Futility," he says, "The Church at first had no buildings, no separated clergy, no set ritual, no bishops, no pope, yet it succeeded in turning life upside down for millions of unknown men and women, giving them a new sense of life's meaning and superb courage in the face of persecution or sorrow. It is our tragedy that we are living in a day when much of this primal force is spent. Once a church was a brave and revolutionary fellowship, changing the course of history by the introduction of discordant ideas: today it is a place where people go and sit on comfortable benches, waiting patiently until time to go home to their Sunday dinners." [73]

Our culture in America and across the world is becoming increasingly hostile towards the Christian faith. Islamic extremist are slaughtering thousands of believers for no other reason other than their faith in Christ. Our own country is openly hostile to the Word of God and has little regard for the Christian foundation our country was based upon. Just a few years ago, it was inconceivable that we could actually be incarcerated for openly declaring God's Word and yet that day is on the horizon. In the not-too-distant-future it will take exceptional courage to minister in Christ's name.

3

Let's End Racial Prejudice Now!

It seems like every day we hear of a new accusation of racism or an incident is referred to as racist. Sometimes well founded and sometimes fueled by the media, there seems to be no end to the hostility between the races which all too often ends in violence. Each year it seems as if the divide between the races gets greater and more volatile. But despite the continually escalating tensions, one thing is certain: the salvation that God provides through Jesus Christ makes it impossible for a true believer to engage in racism or to be considered a racist. Racial prejudices have no place in God's plan.

We must do all we can to stop this division between races—for our community's sake, for our country's sake, for Christ's sake. In a recent article titled, "Racial Reconciliation and the Gospel," Richard Land makes an appeal for an end to these hostilities: "This rift must be healed and healed as quickly as possible because the longer it is left to fester and metastasize, the more alienation and damage is caused, the more difficult it will become to heal, and the more people will be victimized." [74]

As believers, we cannot allow this to happen within our churches. It is well past time to bring an end to judgments based on racial identity. Jesus does not discriminate; the Gospel is for people of every race, from every nation.

In Matthew 28, Jesus tells His disciples, "'All authority has been given to Me in heaven and on earth. Go, therefore, and make disciples of all nations,...'" (Matthew 28:18-19). Notice that there is no discrimination one nation from another. He says to make disciples "of all nations." No one is excluded based on any race or ethnicity. In fact, "of all nations" is literally translated to <u>panta ta ethne</u>, meaning "all the peoples." We get our word ethnic from this phrase which refers to those distinct cultural and racial characteristics that distinguish one people from another.

It is not talking about the nations and political boundaries of our modern world. These are a constantly moving target, affected by political climate, wars, and evolving societal norms. Jesus is talking about every culture and ethnicity of people the world over. Jesus is commissioning us today to make disciples, Christ-like followers, of every ethnic, cultural, and language group in the world.

The plan of God and the passion of God are the same: that all peoples come to know Him. Our mission must be the same. Look at these facts concerning the priority Christ places upon 'the nations' –

- There are more than 800 references to "the nations" in the Bible
- There are approximately 170 references to "grace"
- There are approximately 160 mentions of "salvation"
- There are only 18 times "forgiveness" is found in Scripture
- "Love" is mentioned slightly more than 300 times

What does all this add up to? The references to "the nations" is presented in Scripture more times than grace, salvation, forgiveness, and love combined! It is clear that the heart of God and His passion resides in reaching "the nations" with the Gospel.

John foresaw a day when race, ethnicity, and cultural background wouldn't matter. His prophetic words in The Book of Revelation give no merit to a person's skin color:

> "'...After this I looked, and there was a vast multitude from every nation, tribe, people, and language, which no one could number, standing before the throne of the Lamb...'" –Revelation 7:9

God's mission will be completed. And for this to happen, the Gospel must be preached to all corners of the world so that people from every nation, tribe, and culture come to know Christ.

In the Book of Ephesians, Paul confirms that in salvation we receive redemption and the forgiveness of sins. But there is so much more beyond this sacred promise. We get caught up in focusing on the solution for our need for forgiveness and redemption, but Paul tells us to focus mostly on God.

In Ephesians alone, Paul makes 103 direct references to God, Christ, and Lord. The entire book is filled with God and his manifestations through phrases such as in Him, in His sight, in His will, His grace, His glory, His calling, His inheritance, His power, His blood, His body, He raised us up, His peace, He reconciled, and His riches. Paul wanted to make it clear that salvation is the starting point for believers to know and experience God; not the ending place.

If you ask the average believer what salvation means to them, you'll usually hear phrases related to redemption, the forgiveness of sins, and/or the gift of eternal life. All well and good and true, but by no means, an exhaustive list. The endgame of salvation is not about us; it is all about God. Ephesians reminds us that the goal of our salvation is " to the praise of His glorious grace…" (Ephesians 1:6) and "so that we…might bring praise to His glory (Ephesians 1:12).

We will never fully understand the greatness of salvation unless we have some concept of just how desperate and depraved we were before God intervened. We were not just dead in our sins, we were dead because of them. Not almost dead. Not desperately ill and failing fast. Fully and completely spiritually dead. Before salvation came to each of us, we were essentially evil—living as if God did not even exist, totally outside of His life, and literally dead to all that truly matters.

This is how Paul described the 'before and after' of salvation:

> "And you were dead in your trespasses and sins
> in which you previously walked according to the
> ways of this world, according to the ruler who
> exercises authority over the lower heavens, the
> spirit now working in the disobedient. We too

all previously lived among them in our fleshly desires, carrying out the inclinations of our flesh and thoughts, and we were by nature children under wrath as the others were also. But God..."

–Ephesians 2:1-4

And then the clincher—"But God..." Two wonderful words that bridge the 'before' with the glorious 'after.' The solution to the problem of sinful mankind is revealed: God. We are delivered from the condemnation due us through the holy intervention of Christ. We receive the salvation; God receives glory in the church and in Christ Jesus to all generations forever (Ephesians 3:20-21). As believers, we are the church and embody God's inheritance. It is His purpose to reveal wisdom and grace "through the church to the rulers and authorities in the heavens" (Ephesians 3:10).

Ephesians 2:14 tells us, "For He is our peace..." Some translations even say "He and no other is our peace." This was originally intended to emphasize the peace between the Jews and Gentiles and the peace between believers and God. In ancient times, the world was divided between two main groups: the Jews and the Gentiles. These groups so despised one another that unity between the two seemed almost impossible. Yet, that is exactly what Paul was referring to.

Paul was preaching unity—true unity; not just the absence of conflict. He knew authentic, transformational peace comes from God; only God. Paul was pressing these two distinct groups not just to end the open hostility, but to actually love one another.

Beyond the Ephesians, Paul declared to the Colossians, "'And let the peace of the Messiah, to which you were also called in one body, control your hearts. Be thankful (Colossians 3:15). The literal translation of this is "let the peace of Christ be the umpire or arbitrator between you when disputes arise." That's a great word picture—whenever there's conflict, Christ (or Christ-like behavior) makes the call. When people let the peace of Christ have precedence over every division of every kind, there is peace among the people.

The life and death of Jesus removed all the previous barriers between believers. Whether they be Jew or Gentile, the distinction was secondary to their common belief. Paul explains how the separation was nullified through Christ:

> "He made of no effect the law consisting of commands and expressed in regulations, so that He might create in Himself one new man from the two, resulting in peace. He did this so that He might reconcile both to God in one body through the cross and put the hostility to death by it."
>
> –Ephesians 2:15-16

Jesus's life and ministry was almost exclusively among the Jews. He conformed to the traditions of Judaism and rarely traveled outside the limits of Israel. His first church was made up of Jews and He commanded his disciples to take The Great Commission to the Jews first. The Jewish people were clearly Christ's first love, but not his only love.

Following Stephen's martyrdom, the Apostles were the only believers who remained in Jerusalem. The rest scattered as the persecution spread and began preaching the Gospel to outlying areas. Gentiles began attending the church plants and spreading the news themselves. This was an extremely hard adjustment for many Jewish believers and was reinforced every day as they went to Temple to pray.

Each temple had within it a barrier that separated the Jews from the Gentiles within the House of God. Etched into the wall by each entrance from the Court of the Gentiles was a stone slab warning Gentiles they could not enter under penalty of death. The warning read, "No foreigner may enter within the barricade which surrounds the sanctuary and enclosure. Anyone who is caught doing so will have himself to blame for his ensuing death."

This is exactly what Paul was speaking of when he referred to "the dividing wall of hostility" (Ephesians 2:14) being broken down at the cross. It is a clear reference to the Jewish temple and the various courts it was divided into—Gentile, women, Israel, priests, Holy Place, and the Holy of Holies. Before the crucifixion, the Gentiles were only allowed entrance into the first court.

What makes Paul's words so much more powerful is his strict, blue blood Hebrew heritage. He didn't just think the Jews were superior before his conversion experience, he made it his personal crusade to seek out those Gentiles who were following Christ. However, once Christ entered his heart, the transformation was miraculous as this former zealot begins writing to the people who were formerly pagan Gentiles and approaching them as equals. He is rejoicing with them that they both share the same conversion experience. With Paul and so many others, the impossible became reality at Ephesus; it was proof positive of the effective work of Christ making all things new. Now, Paul was preaching the creation of a new man, one who was neither Jew nor Gentile. He was preaching reconciliation from one man to another and between man and God—and peace coming to all as a result.

When man is consumed by sin, he is deeply divided by many human and spiritual factors: racial and ethnic hatred and distrust, political and social realities, religious disputes, and more. Without a spiritual base, all the issues of the day become relative to him—relative to how they impact him, relative to what he considers right, and relative to what society will bear.

As believers, though, we are co-heirs with Christ Jesus just as the Gentiles were in Paul's day. When we accept the saving grace of the Gospel, we become members of the same body and share in the promise of Jesus just as the early Gentile believers did. These were revolutionary ideas for a society as divided as the Jews and the Gentiles were back then. But Paul was a revolutionary in everything he did. Rather than excluding the Gentiles from God's love and grace, he declares that it was God's eternal purpose all along that they should be fellow heirs, fellow members, and partners in the promise Christ brought to the world.

Today, there is no comparable racial or ethnic barrier equal to what existed between the Jews and the Gentiles. Jews were defiant in their beliefs that Gentiles simply existed outside the love of God. Rabbis even taught that Gentiles were little more than fuel for the fires of hell. Strict Jews wouldn't eat a meal prepared by a Gentile and even went so far as to rinse their utensils before a meal in case they had been touched by a Gentile. And when they returned from the market place, Jews took ceremonial baths in case their clothing accidentally touch a Gentile.

The disdain the Jews held for the Gentiles while Paul was alive was blatant; their actions extreme. And while it was unkind and uncaring, it was mostly just done in obedience to their intense beliefs. So when Paul began welcoming Gentiles into the church treating them as brothers, and showing respect, it took the supernatural power of Christ to help the Jews accept Christ's unconditional love of all. As Jew and Gentile believers began living, working, and worshipping together in peace, it was evident they had become a new creation—followers united "in Christ." Like the believers of old, the divisions and chaos among us today can only be solved when we identify ourselves as being "in Christ" and not by racial, ethnic, or political labels.

Dr. Leo Day is Dean of the Church Music School at Southwestern Seminary. He is also African American. About a year ago, Dr. Day and I led worship at First Baptist Church, Jackson, Mississippi. It was a wonderful time of celebration that wouldn't have happened many decades ago. The church is historic because close to 60 years ago they tried to fire their white pastor for trying to bring black people into the church. Fortunately, the pastor remained, the objections diminished, and the church worked to overcome their prejudices.

To Christ's glory that Sunday, Dr. Day and I were both there, side by side, as new creations of Jesus Christ where there is no bond or freedom, no rich or poor, no educated or illiterate, and no racial or cultural differences. That is true only in Christ!

We are all called into one body and have been created as new individuals in Christ. The result is that we are brothers or sisters in Christ, regardless of our skin color or cultural heritage. When we recognize fellow believers as being "in Christ" as we are "in Christ," we can forgive and forget and move past the racial differences and divisions that stand in the way of others. We can join hands together as we are all in Christ knowing ours is an eternity together.

No matter how different from our cultural norm or how unique a culture's practices, there are no races, nations, lands, or people outside the love and mercy of God. Every ethnicity, every tribe, group, and culture will be included before His throne.

My life has been immeasurably blessed by friends the world over, from many different nationalities and from every continent. I count these friends as cherished partners in ministry. In fact, one Sunday while I was pastor at First Baptist Church, Euless, I counted nine different nationalities in our choir alone. Early in my ministry I have had staff and church members from ethnic minorities in leadership in the churches where I have served.

Our lives are richer when we move past racial prejudices, cultural distinctions, and critical stereotypes and embrace each other as fellow heirs of the unmerited, yet richly abundant grace of God. To live anyway else is not Christ honoring. We have allowed racism to divide us for too long, sometimes to the point of convincing others it is compatible with the Gospel. Nothing could be further from the truth! We must declare what the Bible reveals: every individual in the world is of eternal worth, made in the image of God (Genesis 1:27).

The time has long since arrived that we must bridge every gap that exists between races—all races! Formally, the resolutions of our conventions have asked forgiveness from our African American brothers. Now we must work within our churches and communities to completely eradicate all racism, no matter how ingrained in the culture it is. Let us declare, "Enough is enough!" and help to usher in the day when Martin Luther King's dream becomes a reality and people "will not be judged by the color of their skin but by the content of their character."

Always Share Your Faith

The cries of a lost world resound with a deafening and thunderous roar. Never before has there been so much devastation and despair in the hearts of individuals as today. Never before have so many enjoyed so much of the tangible things of this world yet the despair and hopelessness in the human heart is greater than it has ever been. The hurts of so many lost people cry out for our attention.

More than 100 years ago J. Wilbur Chapman made the appeal for Christian character in his book, "The Pastor His Own Evangelist:" "Let the pastor clearly grasp the fact that the moment the spiritual life of the church is toned up, all the conditions for a general religious awakening will be present. There is no evangelism like that of Christian character. Once let the church throw off the spirit of selfish indifference to the welfare of the world and the world will know it and respond to it." [75]

Euangelion is the Greek word from which we get evangelism. It means to preach the Gospel that is revealed to us in the Bible. It refers not only to the content of what is preached, but also the act and process and execution of the proclamation. In regards to evangelism, the content and the process of preaching are one, not to be separated. The preaching of the Gospel is inspired; it is quite literally, "God's power for salvation to everyone who believes…" (Romans 1:16).

What is the Gospel but the story of Christ forsaking all for us. In His supreme wisdom, God has acted for the salvation of the world through Jesus Christ. Through His incarnation as a human, His human death, and miraculous resurrection, Jesus made possible eternal life. He became sin for each of us, dying in our place to pay the penalty for our sins. He died a very real death, was buried in a tomb, and rose again on the third day. He was victorious over the grave, ascended to heaven, and will one day return to establish His eternal Kingdom upon the earth. Each of us must make the decision to turn from our sins and trust Him as Lord and Savior by faith. This is the message of the Gospel.

We are commissioned to share the Gospel wherever we go. The great missionary Robert Speer took this to heart when he said, "You say you have faith? Well, then, either give it out or give it up." Faith is personal but never intended to be kept private.

My phone rang one morning at 2 a.m. and the police officer on the other end said they had just arrested a woman who insisted on speaking to me. She had attended our church, but was not a member. Turns out, she had gone to a bar and been picked up by a man. Over the course of the evening, they both became drunk and he left her in a parking lot, stranded and abused. She had called to cry out because she felt lonely and abandoned. Her cry to me was, "Please! Help me!" She didn't want to go on living like she was.

Another evening, Carol Ann and I were about to leave to make some visitation calls when I received a call from a Dallas police detective. He explained that in a nearby apartment complex in Euless a man had barricaded himself into his apartment. Apparently, the man had a gun and had threatened anyone who came near. The man had asked to speak to me.

We went immediately to the apartment complex and found it surrounded by SWAT teams from nearby police departments. They allowed me access past the crime scene barricade and into the man's apartment. Inside, I found a 70-year-old man with a .38 caliber pistol in his lap. He was overcome by loneliness and had lost his will to live. His wife had died and his children had abandoned him and he was crying out for help. He didn't really want to die; he just wanted to know someone cared about him.

These are two very dramatic stories of people going to extremes to cry out for help. But all day, every day, people are crying out in less obvious ways. Everyone around you is crying out for help of some sort. Those without Christ are crying in desperation and helplessness and need the hope we have as believers. Paul experienced this call for help first hand when it came to him in a vision and "...A Macedonian man was standing and pleading with him, 'Cross over to Macedonia and help us!'" (Acts 16:9). We may not have the visions of Paul, but the world is still calling out for help.

Christ is the only hope for the darkness of the world today. No other force can save our fallen world. As believers, we are called to oppose the forces of evil around us. Whether they be terrorists in another part of the world making their way towards us or the continued disintegration of truth, morality, and ethics in our country, the world is coming for us and against us and we must share our faith with all we meet.

Charles L. Goddell emphatically shares the calling we all have to share the Good News in "Heralds of a Passion." He says, "How can any of us dare to represent Christ to men if we do not know something of the thrill of Hiss passion, if we do not yearns after the souls of men so that we can cry concerning our own flock, as John Knox cried for Scotland, 'Give me Scotland, or I die!' This and no other is the passion which has transformed the world." [76] The Southern Baptist Convention is baptizing less people each year than we did in 1954, despite the fact that our membership now numbers 16 million versus six million then. But don't be discouraged by the numbers. Consider this: if every pastor won one person a month to Christ, we would baptize more than half a million people in one year!

We are all guilty of not sharing our faith enough. Whether pastor or member, we are all called to share the Gospel with the lost world. If we continue along this path, we will become a disappearing people. As it stands, we are already a shrinking minority in our own land. At the current rate of attrition among believers, my great-grandchildren will live in a country of only 4% believers. We have to bring light to the darkness of our country and the world if our faith is to survive.

Charles Spurgeon made an impassioned plea for believers to engage those around them in an article from long ago. In it he said, "If sinners be damned, at least let them leap to hell over our bodies. And if they perish, let them perish with our arms about their knees, imploring them to stay. If hell must be filled, at least let it be filled in the teeth of our exertions, and let no one go there unwarned and unprayed for." [77] We must see ourselves as those entrusted with a secret that we have to tell; as stewards of God's mysteries that we must share.

Keep a Good Sense of Humor and Laugh at Yourself

3

One of the best things you can do in your ministry is to learn to laugh at yourself. It's really not that hard and goes a long way towards building relationships with those you serve. I have had plenty of opportunities to practice this through the years and it has never yet failed me.

When I became president of the Sunday School Board of the Southern Baptist Convention, Dr. James Sullivan was still active in Nashville. He had been president of the Sunday School Board many years before for some 23 years and was greatly loved across our convention. He gave me lots of friendly advice through the years and I came to cherish every nugget of wisdom he shared. I've never forgotten one priceless piece of advice he gave me and that was, "Take your job seriously; yourself never!"

When things happen in your life that are funny, share them with those you minister with and minister to. Sometimes crazy things just happen that are hilarious!

Sometimes, they're even our own fault! Either way, I have found that laughter is good medicine for crazy mishaps and an excellent tonic for discouragement and despair. Don't get sensitive; get to sharing and laughing.

Proverbs tells us of the good that comes from "a joyful heart:"

"A joyful heart makes a face cheerful,
but a sad heart produces a broken spirit."
–Proverbs 15:13

"All the days of the oppressed are miserable,
but a cheerful heart has a continual feast."
–Proverbs 15: 15

"A joyful heart is good medicine,
but a broken spirit dries up the bones."
–Proverbs 17:22

Those are strong testimonials for having a joyful heart. When the options are laughing or sulking or crying, the Bible is clear: joyfulness wins every time.

My family is having a field day with me these days as my hearing continues to fail. I have become very dependent upon my hearing aids to the point I can hardly hear without them. If there is a lot of background noise or outside sounds around me, it makes it very difficult for me to hear correctly. If my overall failing hearing wasn't enough, I also have a hearing disability that doesn't allow me to hear consonants well. Someone might say 'rake' that I hear as 'gate' or 'go' that sounds like 'no' to me. As you can imagine, it can be very confusing at times.

When I've asked the doctor about my hearing issues, he tells me that I am hearing with my brain. If I hear a sound, I use my brain to try and figure out what it is. This causes me to delay responding or misunderstand what was said. It has made for some humorous conversations as I've answered questions that weren't even asked and offered comments on things totally unrelated!

Still, as bad as my hearing may be at times, I hope it never gets as bad this couple:

In visiting with her husband, the wife told him, "I'm proud of you!"

The husband mistakenly replied, "I'm tired of you, too!"

My family still laughs at the funny comments I've made as my hearing has left me. And you know what? I laugh with them because a good sense of humor is good medicine for us all!

3 Manage Your Time Well

The one thing we all share is the amount of time we have each and every day. No matter our profession, our hobbies, our responsibilities, we're all given the same 24 hours a day every time the clock strikes midnight. The difference between people who accomplish much and impact others is how they discipline themselves in regards to their time.

I have found it helps to have a daily routine for the most important things. This helps you from becoming sidetracked by the urgent. Although the urgent issues are often the squeakiest wheel, they are rarely the most important. You have to be available for real emergencies, but also disciplined enough to take care of the necessities each day including time with God, preparation for your message, time with family, staff and administrative responsibilities, and shepherding the flock you've been given.

The Bible has a lot to say about time—how we spend ours, God's timing, the End Times, and much more. These are just a few of the verses that speak of time:

> "Our steps were closely followed so that we could not walk in our streets. Our end drew near; our time ran out. Our end had come!"
>
> – Lamentations 4:18

"...for still the end will come at the appointed time...At the appointed time...until the time of the end, for it will still come at the appointed time." –Daniel 11:27, 29,35

"But you, Daniel, keep these words secret and seal the book until the time of the end...for the words are secret and sealed until the time of the end."
–Daniel 12:4, 9

"Pay careful attention, then, to how you walk—not as unwise people but as wise—making the most of the time, because the days are evil."
–Ephesians 5:15-16

"Act wisely toward outsiders, making the most of the time." –Colossians 4:5

It is time for us to seek the Lord:
"Sow righteousness for yourselves
and reap faithful love;
break up your unplowed ground.
It is time to seek the Lord
until He comes and sends righteousness
on you like the rain."
–Hosea 10:12

"It is time for the Lord to act,
for they have violated Your instruction."
–Psalms 119:126

It is time to wake out of sleep:
"Besides this, knowing the time, it is already the
hour for you to wake up from sleep, for now our
salvation is nearer than when we first believed."
–Romans 13:11

"And I say this, brothers: The time is limited…"
–I Corinthians 7:29

"Mordecai told the messenger to reply to Esther, '…
Who knows, perhaps you have come to your royal
position for such a time as this.'"
– Esther 4:13, 14

We are called to make the most of our time—to use this
limited and most valuable resource to the best of our abilities.
This is one of the most crucial areas of our ministries. Moses'
experience with the burning bush is an excellent example
of responding to the Lord's timing. Here is the account in
Exodus:

"Then the Angel of the Lord appeared to him in a
flame of fire within a bush. As Moses looked, he
saw that the bush was on fire but was not consume.

So Moses thought: I must go over and look at this remarkable sight. Why isn't the bush burning up?

When the Lord saw that he had gone over to look, God called out to him from the bush, 'Moses, Moses!'

'Here I am,' he answered."

–Exodus 3:2-4

Just think for a moment how the course of history—of our very faith—would have been altered had Moses not stopped what he was doing to respond to this remarkable sight. God would never have spoken to him in this way, challenged him to lead His people out of Egypt, and the legacy of the Israelites would be forever altered. Whenever, wherever, and however the Lord comes to us, we must stop to hear His voice and prayerfully follow His lead.

That's not to say that Moses had an easy time of it, persuading the Israelites to follow him, just because he was following God's call. It was difficult and demanding to him, but God honored Moses' obedience throughout this adventure. When faced with the opportunity to enter the Promised Land, the very land the Lord had set aside for them, the Israelites chose to believe the words of their brothers over the words of the Lord, despite Moses' appeals. When they eventually realized the Lord's plan was sovereign and they should have followed Him in the first place, the time had passed for their obedience and the Lord's consequences were near. Hear the anguish in Moses' words as he explains the error of their ways to the Israelites:

"When Moses reported these words to all the Israelites, the people were overcome with grief. They got up early the next morning and went up the ridge of the hill country, saying, 'Let's go to the place the Lord promised, for we were wrong.'

"But Moses responded, 'Why are you going against the Lord's command? It won't succeed. Don't go, because the Lord is not among you and you will be defeated by your enemies...since you have turned from following Him.'"

–Numbers 14:39-43

It was too little, too late for the Israelites—they had rebelled against God when He commanded them to enter the land He had promised them and they had missed the time God set apart for their obedience. There is a lesson for all of us in their misconduct: managing our time effectively and efficiently is vital to our relationship with the Lord and in the ministry he has assigned to each of us. When He calls, we are to respond obediently and in His time.

This is God's time for us. Daily, the world further unravels as violence, promiscuity, hatred, and godlessness grow exponentially. We knew these times were to come—that's no surprise—but now is the time for us to respond to God's call if we are to slow this destructive course. So much of what Paul told Timothy has been realized and continues to strengthen its grasp on our country and our world. Paul's words are just as relevant now as they were then:

"But know this: Difficult times will come in the last days. For people will be lovers of self, lovers of money, boastful, proud, blasphemers, disobedient to parents, ungrateful, unholy, unloving, irreconcilable, slanderers, without self-control, brutal, without love for what is good, traitors, reckless, conceited, lovers of pleasure rather than lovers of God, holding to the form of godliness but denying its power..." –II Timothy 3:1-5

When we read these ancient words, it is as if Paul is here among us now, witnessing the degradation of our communities, country, and world. And while the decline is severe, we are not without hope. And abilities. And time. Time is the greatest tool we have in our ministries. Let us not abuse, misuse, squander, or waste what precious time we have been given to make the greatest impact we can. If we don't manage our time, it will manage us! Establishing our priorities is the key step to best managing our time.

Johnny Hunt explains this well in "Building Your Spiritual Resume:" "Life is full of problems, full of potential but devoid of proper priorities. Priorities are simply the precedents you set for life. Priorities deal with how you arrange life. Those things that are significant to you are your priorities. Significant factors are established by your walk rather than your talk." [78]

If we make it a priority to set our priorities and follow through with action, we are maximizing our strengths and affecting the most people for the best cause: Christ.

3   Give Clear Directions and Expectations

It is to everyone's advantage when you minimize ambiguity and obscurity. If you have to err between being quick and over-communicating, it is always best to make sure your expectations are clearly established. Clear and concise communication is the key to helping people succeed. Your staff and your members need to understand what the key issues are facing your church and the factors involved in making decisions about them. When you are forth coming with all the pertinent information, people are much more likely to support you wholeheartedly, free of doubt and reservations.

To lead well, you must communicate well. My brother sent me a plaque that captures the way many of us sometime communicate. It says:

"I know you believe you understand what you think I said. But I am not sure you realize that what you heard is not what I meant."

Isn't this the way it is sometimes when we talk with others? I say something, but my friend hears it differently. They think they understand what was said, but it in no way resembles what I meant. Sometimes these misunderstandings can be humorous; sometimes tragic.

Oftentimes, we take too much for granted, assuming others hear and understand what we say and what we mean.

As ministers, this is critically important. It is far too easy to assume others with whom we minister know all that we do and why we do it. We assume they have all the facts we have, all the input we've heard, and all the resources made available to us and frequently, they don't. When this happens, we tend to skip a lot of valuable and clear explanations because everything is so obvious to us. Never make this assumption. Always make sure others understand what you mean to say to them.

I had the opportunity to practice this lesson in extensive communicating when we went to back-to-back Sunday School and Worship services at First Baptist Church, Euless. We took a full year to explain the rationale for the decision, the expectations from the decision, and what would be required to make a successful change involving using all our facilities twice on Sunday morning.

As part of the process, we met with and informed all the leadership teams all that was involved in this transition. We came to each meeting with all the information we had used to reach this decision. Then we systematically met with all the adult and youth Bible study departments as well as the adult workers in each of the children's areas. In every instance, we responded to questions and concerns as best we could and related the way the proposal was presented for their consideration and implementation.

We realized going into this arrangement that the split to two hours of worship and Bible Study required a 50/50 split in attendance between the service times. Anything significantly less than that would require a long look at the value of making such a big decision. After a year of intentionally clear and concise, but very inclusive information, we made the move to two worship services and two Sunday School times. The result was virtually perfect and exceeded our expectations of success. I fully attribute this to the extensive efforts we made in advance to inform and educate our people.

I have found that people can be led to do almost anything church leadership desires if clear communication and rationale is provided. This must be provided for every significant decision a church makes. As ministers, it is our task to make every aspect of all major issues completely transparent. When people understand the rationale and the goals of the issues, they usually respond positively. It is when communication is not clear and expectations are obscure that confusion and conflict arise among the people. Make it an everyday practice to communicate in such a manner that there is no room for misunderstanding or misconceptions. In doing so, you will develop trust and enjoy the support of your people.

Have a Positive Attitude

3

Always have an upbeat, excited, and energetic attitude or what my son, Randy, calls a "happy to do it" attitude. It can affect everything about you—your outlook, your words and actions and thoughts, and others' response to you as well. Attitude is everything.

Robert Jeffress speaks of the importance of attitude in his book, "Choose Your Attitudes, Change Your Life:" "God's Sovereign purpose is to change us into the image of His Son. Yet, we can choose to allow life circumstances either to strengthen us or to destroy us. The determining factor is our attitude. Here is a good definition of attitude: Attitude is our mental and emotional response to the circumstances of life. We may not be able to change many of our circumstances, but we can change our attitudes." [79]

In my experiences, I have found that enthusiasm can inspire and gain support quickly. Your enthusiasm is literally contagious! Whatever it is you undertake for the Lord, personally or corporately in your church, do so with excitement and enthusiasm. Charles L. Goodell knew the value of wholehearted effort when he said, "The fiercest enemy to be fought in our day is sheer apathy." [80]

We have the greatest message in the world inside our hearts and minds and souls! We shouldn't be half-hearted when we speak of what Jesus has done for us. We have the most blessed privilege in all the world to be ministers for God. It is imperative that we are not apathetic towards this sacred opportunity. Pour your heart into your ministry with enthusiasm and your spirit will spill over and spread quickly. Let your energy be channeled into the ministry of the Lord with excitement and enthusiasm and God will greatly bless you.

In "A Guide to Preachers," Alfred E. Garvie captures the need for impassioned preaching: "The power of preaching depends on passion, the intensity of the emotion which the truth itself inspired in the preacher. There must not only be light, but heat also. A sermon delivered in an unimpassioned way, as though the preacher cared not at all either for his message or for the reception his hearers might give to it, cannot be an effective sermon." [81]

The life of King Hezekiah shows a man passionate about correcting wrongs when it concerns his faith. Unlike his father, Ahaz, one of Judah's most wicked kings, Hezekiah trusted the Lord throughout his 29-year reign. He introduced radical reforms such as removing the pagan high places of worship, destroying idolatrous symbols, and centralizing worship in Jerusalem. The sacred historian who wrote II Kings gives him the highest commendation in saying,

> "Hezekiah trusted in the Lord God of Israel; not one of the kings of Judah was like him, either before him or after him. He remained faithful to Yahweh and did not turn from following Him but kept the commands the Lord had commanded Moses. The Lord was with him, and wherever he went he prospered…" –II Kings 18:5-7

Although he inherited vassal status from Ahaz, Hezekiah openly and aggressively rebelled against the pagan powers that oppressed his country. So much so that his defiance led to the invasion of the Assyrians by Sennacharib. The story, told in Isaiah 36-38 and II Kings 18-19, tells of 185,000 Assyrians being killed by the angel of the Lord in a remarkable deliverance. Hezekiah listened to Isaiah, petitioned God for deliverance, and received a remarkable victory as a result. Still jubilant from victory, Hezekiah became deathly ill and the Lord sent a messenger to him, preparing him to die.

The Scripture says:

> "…The prophet Isaiah son of Amoz came and said to him, This is what the Lord says: 'Put your affairs in order, for you are about to die; you will not recover.'" –Isaiah 38:1

Hezekiah's first response was to turn his face to the wall and pray. Eastern houses of the day would usually have ottomans or couches running alongside of the outside wall. For Hezekiah, his turning to the wall was an instinctive expression that he was alone with God in this bitter moment. He was tormented and in denial about dying in the prime of his life.

In desperation, Hezekiah made an impassioned plea to God for reasons to extend his life. In the middle of his anguish, he stops to remind God how he had "wholeheartedly" walked before God. This is his prayer:

"...Please, Lord, remember how I have walked before You faithfully and wholeheartedly, and have done what pleases You...."

Hezekiah knew the power of what he was saying and asking of the Lord. He knew his claims of wholeheartedness in the Hebrew language meant he was of pure heart and singularly focused, and that his devotion was without defect, and found to be sound and sincere. And God's response was to extend his life by 15 years.

Just like Hezekiah, we are to follow the Lord wholeheartedly—with wholehearted enthusiasm for Him and the ministry He has given to each of us. For God's sake and your sake, don't serve the Lord half-heartedly as if you are merely going through the motions of obedience. Give Him your whole heart and keep your eyes fast upon Him. Serve the Lord with all your heart, mind, and soul and with spirited enthusiasm!

Meet People on Their Turf

3

Most people are usually more comfortable at their home, their office, or some place they are familiar with. Keep that in mind when you meet with people outside of your office and make every effort to meet where they are most comfortable. As servant leaders, this is an excellent way to place their preferences above ours.

We are to serve the people God places in and around us just as Jesus did with His disciples when He washed their feet. He humbled Himself by coming to earth from heaven and He humbled himself when He went to the cross. To be like Christ, we are to humble ourselves before those we serve and sometimes this means meeting them where they are most comfortable. It's easy to forget that the people we work with day in and day out, our staffs and active volunteers, are of great worth and value. When we always ask them to come to our office instead of considering going to theirs is to imply that we are more important than they are. We would never say that naturally, but the simple act of meeting them on their turf speaks volumes about the trust and value we have in them.

One of my strongest emphases when I served as president of LifeWay was my relationship with the State Executive Directors of the various state conventions. These men were some of my closest friends and allies in the ministry we shared with the churches across our convention. One day it occurred to me that, while I knew most of them very well,

I had never gone to their offices to ask how we might serve with them better. They came to our LifeWay offices every December for a time of sharing over a couple of days and I hosted a special banquet for them at each Southern Baptist convention. But I realized it wasn't the same as sitting down in their offices, on their turf, allowing them to share their heart with me about what was important to them and how we could help them.

Right then, I determined to go and see each one of them, one by one, with the trip dedicated solely to seeing each one of them personally. I didn't stack one trip on top of another or schedule trips back to back so as to visit one 'while I was in the area' seeing another. I wanted to convey to them that they were important and each one warranted a trip dedicated to them. It took me 103 days and two years to complete, but it was the best thing I ever did for my relationship with them. These men were and remain gifted and devoted leaders and some of my very best friends; I wanted them to know they were of value to me, so I went to them.

This same practice works on a much smaller scale even within your own office. By taking the time to go to others' offices, you're conveying respect to them by saying they're important enough to come to. I did this frequently in all my churches and at LifeWay just to make the point. It even has a name—MBWA, or Ministry By Walking Around. It is a tremendously simple gesture that says so much to those you work with.

I took this practice out of the office and extended it to getting to know the deacons in the churches where I served. I visited each one of their homes when I first came to be their pastor for no other reason than to tell them I loved them, prayed for them, and wanted to serve them as pastor. To this day, my closest friends beyond the company of pastors and preachers I know well, are deacons I have served with through the years.

When you make the effort to make others comfortable, you are helping them to be at their best in ministry and strengthening your relationship. You're not just telling them they are significant to you and the ministry; you are showing them, too.

Learn to Delegate

No matter how well you multitask, you will never be able to do all that needs to be done in your ministry. You can't do it all and you shouldn't try. This is where it is important to empower others to serve and to trust them with significant responsibility. Train your people in the areas where they are needed and help them to develop their gifts and talents. Even though you could do a task quicker in the short term, lasting success and staff engagement comes from developing others within your ministry.

Paul knew first hand that no one person could tend to all the needs of a growing ministry. In preaching to the

Ephesians, he shared God's grand design for gifting each of us differently:

> "And He personally gave some to be apostles, some prophets, some evangelists, some pastors and teachers, for the training of the saints in the work of ministry, to build up the body of Christ,…"
>
> –Ephesians 4:11-12

God didn't give any one man all of these gifts; He gave specific gifts and talents so the responsibilities could be shared and done by those best suited for each task. He never intended for one man to fulfill all these roles, but rather for each of us to do what we do best and that to which we are called, all for the sake of the Body of Christ.

W. A. Criswell knew well the power of investing and delegating. He often told me when we served together, "I cannot put my arms around everybody, but I can put my arms around a few. And they can put their arms around some more, and it continues until everybody has somebody's arms around them." That is a perfect picture of how delegation works.

Moses gave one of the first lessons in delegation in the Book of Exodus. Here is the account from Exodus 18:

"When Moses' father-in-law saw everything he was doing for them he asked, 'What is this thing you're doing for the people? Why are you alone siting as judge, while all the people stand around you from morning until evening?'

"Moses replied to his father-in-law, 'Because the people come to me to inquire of God. Whenever they have a dispute, it comes to me, and I make a decision between one man and another. I teach them God's statutes and laws.'

"'What you are doing is not good,' Moses' father-in-law said to him. 'You will certainly wear out both yourself and these people who are with you, because the task is too heavy for you. You can't do it alone. Now listen to me; I will give you some advice, and God be with you. You be the one to represent the people before God and bring their cases to Him. Instruct them about the statues and laws, and teach them the way to live and what they must do. But you should select from all the people able men, God-fearing, trustworthy, and hating bribes. Place them over the people as commanders of thousands, hundreds, fifties, and tens. They should judge the people at all times. Then they can bring you every important case but judge every minor case themselves. In this way you will lighten your load, and they will bear it with you. If you do this, and God so directs you, you will be able to endure, and also all these people will be able to go home satisfied'" (Exodus 18:14-23).

The lesson Moses' father-in-law shared with him is at least as relevant today as it was thousands of years ago—probably more so. Never before have there been so many distractions before us, each one demanding our time and attention, all the while the responsibilities of pastors increase daily. One of our primary responsibilities should be to train others to serve and then delegate to them opportunities to put this training to use. In doing so, we exponentially expand the potential for others to learn of Christ.

3

Write Notes of Concern, Consolation, and Appreciation

I had a tremendous advantage growing up in a pastor's home. It blessed me in more ways than I could ever begin to realize. In essence, it gave me a front row seat to watch my parents model what a Christian marriage should be. I saw the good times and the challenging ones including raising three boys and changing ministry assignments.

My father was the kind of man who brought people together. He had that special ability to help people see things from others' perspective and break down walls of resistance. I think every congregation he served had a divided congregation at some point that he reconciled.

He modeled so many things for me as a man, a husband, father, and pastor. One of the most remarkable things he did was to write notes of gratitude and encouragement to individuals. It was a small act, but it made a big impact on so many! This made a lasting impression on me and I have done the same thing throughout my life. It has proven to be one of the best ministry tools available as it allows me to connect quickly and personally with those I meet daily. Whether staff members, church members, or just those who cross your path throughout the course of a day, the impact of a handwritten note or a personal email can affect people greatly.

Here are just a few of my personal experiences:

- I made it a practice to write birthday notes to every member, including children, in every church I served until the number grew above 2,000. At that point, it was more than I could do and still meet my other responsibilities. I changed the writing of my notes to include my staff and families, deacons and their families, and key leaders within the church.

- During my time at LifeWay, I wrote every employee who worked in the Nashville office, some 1,700 employees, a birthday note every year for 15 years.

- One year while serving at First Baptist Church, Euless, I took the better part of a month to write a personal note to every family, asking for their involvement in a special church-wide project.

- I also regularly wrote everyone who participated in worship services in a special way. If they sang a solo, gave a testimony, or shared a special message, I wrote them a note every time they participated. Every time someone gave us something personally or encouraged us in our ministry, I wrote them a note.

- Whenever I got a baby announcement, I sent a special letter to the newborn, welcoming them into our world, talking about their parents, the beauty of our world, and the opportunity they would have to learn about Jesus as they grew up. Even though it was really for the parents' benefit at the time, these notes have come to be cherished and appreciated by these children as they have grown up.

- For every graduation announcement I received, I wrote each young person a note of encouragement concerning their future. As deaths occurred, I wrote a condolence note to the remaining spouse and usually the children.

- Whenever I travel to speak, there are always lots of people to thank—those who invited me, those who host me and take care of the travel details. If it is at a church, I send a word of appreciation to the pastor and every staff and support staff member I meet while there. Everyone, no matter their role, likes to be recognized and thanked for their efforts.

The opportunities to encourage and show appreciation to people around you are virtually endless. Nothing, short of a personal visit, makes the impact of a handwritten note to someone. When you send a personal note to someone, it is a reminder to them of your friendship and ministry to them. And while a note in advance of meeting with someone is nice, a follow-up note is always appreciated.

Notes of appreciation also go a long way to making visitors and prospects feel welcome in your church. I used to write a handwritten note to every family or individual that visited one of our services. I also sent follow-up notes to anyone I met on visitation or who I had the privilege of witnessing to.

Every time I left the city to preach or visit elsewhere, I sent a personal note of welcome and encouragement to those I had met. I sent postcards from all over the world to prospects to let them know about our church. It wasn't uncommon for people to come forward to join our church while holding the postcard I had sent them.

I say all this to encourage you to use every means possible to connect with people. Phone calls, emails, and especially handwritten notes—all are great ways to build relationships. When you are people-focused, you find all types of ways to encourage others.

3

Every Church Needs Regular Financial Audits

Every church should have a full financial outside audit conducted every year. It is important for you and your staff to offer full disclosure and accountability to your members. Without it, your members will not have confidence in how the funds are being spent and will not continue to give.

There's a simple test to determine if church funds should be used for a purchase: if it cannot stand up against the scrutiny of an outside audit, it should not be spent. Sadly, this area of financial responsibility is often neglected in many churches and the church suffers for it.

Additionally, every church account should require two signatures for the protection of everyone who handles the church's money. Without the necessary two signatures, it is an invitation for financial disaster for individuals and the church.

I had a first-hand experience of this when I was a young pastor. Our church had the largest kindergarten in the city. It was especially popular because the public schools in our area had not yet begun to offer kindergarten. We had one woman, our Kindergarten treasurer, in charge of all the school's financial transactions. She collected the fees, paid the bills, tended to all the bookkeeping for the school and was the only signature on the checks.

As a rule, our teachers would regularly cash their checks at a nearby grocery store for convenience. When the store quit cashing the teachers' checks due to insufficient funds, I asked the kindergarten director about it. She seemed as perplexed as I was until a little further investigating revealed that large sums of money intended for the kindergarten account were never deposited. As the Kindergarten Treasurer was the only one collecting and depositing the checks and cash, it soon became apparent that she was not handling the funds appropriately and had stolen large amounts from the church over a period of several years. Though the activity was hers, we had placed her in this situation by only requiring one signature on all transactions and by not having an annual audit in place.

When I called the chairman of our Personnel Committee, who was also a very successful businessman, to tell him the situation, he said, "Preacher, you and I ought to have our butts kicked for letting this happen." And he was right—we should never allowed one person to have complete control over all the Kindergarten funds.

We went forward with the investigation, but only reviewed the previous three years. In that time she had taken enough of the church's funds to buy a brand, new car—a serious amount of money! I learned a valuable lesson from this experience: how a church handles its finances is vitally important. It is a valuable trust that your members are putting in you when they give financially.

They are trusting you and your staff to handle their tithes and offerings with integrity. The best way to do this is to have strong financial policies and procedures in place with safeguards to protect everyone who handles church funds in any way. Audits, preferably outside audits, also help insure the record keeping is accurate and honest. However finances are handled in your church, it should be done with accountability and regular outside oversight to protect you and your staff.

3 Be an Advocate for Your Co-Workers

Whenever possible, be an advocate for your ministerial and support staff. Be their biggest supporter and always start out on their side when issues arise. Take the lead with the personnel committee of your church by carefully researching best practices in terms of their salaries and benefits. Make it a practice to encourage the committee to provide at least cost of living raises annually, if not more. Full benefits packages are also an extremely important part of your staff's compensation.

If you are proactive and supportive when it comes to advocating for your staff's salary and benefits, it is likely the personnel committee will do likewise when they review your compensation package. Paul told Timothy that "Elders who are good leaders should be considered worthy of an ample honorarium" (1 Timothy 5:17). Other translations say "worthy of double honor" (NIV). The reference to "honorarium" or "honor" does not merely refer to compensation, but the failure to give appropriate compensation would imply a lack of honor. (New American Commentary) They are on the very front lines of Kingdom work in what is sometimes a thankless job; those who faithfully serve should be honored and compensated as such.

By leading the way in the processes of providing for your staff, you are giving the strong message that the staff and pastor stand together and speak with one voice. This unity goes a long way towards engaging your staff's full support for the direction of the ministry. Without such unity, it can prove to be dangerous to the church's welfare and hazardous to the commission God has given you, the staff, and the church.

Sadly, as much as 95% of church problems are staff problems. Discord, jealousy, even turf wars over the hierarchy of ministries served are just a few of the possible areas for discontent that leads to disloyalty and lack of unity.

Always lead your staff carefully and intentionally. Brag on them every chance you get and let them know you are proud of them and grateful to be serving alongside of them. Always build them up in the eyes of the congregation and never criticize them publicly.

Share the credit for team projects, taking time to acknowledge individuals for their specific contributions and their part in the project's success. Speak of their accomplishments and efforts to your members. Publicly praise them and celebrate the special talents they bring to their service for Christ.

When you advocate for your team, you are letting them know you don't take their time and talents for granted. You are telling them, privately and corporately, that they are an important part of the church's success and what they bring to the ministry is of great worth. Your regular words of affirmation can change mediocre effort into tremendous effort and everyone will be the better for it—especially the church and God's people.

3 Dealing with the Search Committee

There are a handful of things to remember when you are preparing to meet with a Pastor Search Committee, sometimes it is the Personnel Committee, about a new position. First, remember the old saying, "You only have one chance to make a good first impression." It's been passed on for generations because it's true and always will be. Keep this in mind whenever you are meeting with members of a search committee. Be sure to dress neatly and appropriately for the meeting. I used to always check with the contact committee member in advance to find out the dress code. As a rule, it is better to arrive overdressed than underdressed.

If they suggest coat and tie, show up in a coat and tie; if it is business casual, slacks and a sport coat is acceptable. Whatever you decide to wear, present yourself as your best self—clean-shaven or with neatly trimmed facial hair, trimmed nails, and ample deodorant. Take the effort to make an excellent first impression.

Through the years, it has been my experience to realize that the search committee usually doesn't really represent their church. They think they do, and will tell you they do, but don't assume the rest of the church feels as they do. I know of many instances where pastor friends were told one thing by the search committee assigned to bring them to the church only to come to find out they were not representative of the membership at large.

This is precisely why you should never make major changes when you go to a new church quickly. Take the time to get to know the people within the church and other key leaders before you seriously consider such changes. When you meet with anyone regarding a potential position, be prepared for lots of questions. People somehow feel as if they have clearance to ask anything about anything. Don't feel like you have to answer overly intrusive questions, but be open and honest with all you do answer. You should expect questions concerning your leadership philosophy, your music preference, your theological position on virtually everything, plus lots more.

It's also a good idea to ask your contact person if there are any hot buttons or sensitive issues you either need to address or deflect. If they ask you something you're not sure of, a simple, "I don't know," should be sufficient.

Do your homework before visiting with the committee and other church members. Read all you can about the church—its history, its presence in the community, its reputation. Ask for any background information available and read everything available online. The church's website can give you valuable information regarding how the church positions itself, what they see as priorities, and their organizational structure. This can also allow you to learn the names of key staff members in advance of your visit.

It is especially helpful to ask your contact person if there are any unresolved difficulties in the church or within the staff. Many times search committees are looking to a new pastor to come in and solve these problems, however, this is not how it should be done. Known conflicts and problems should be solved and resolved before you come.

Respectfully, tell the search committee that these issues need to be handled before you come. This is particularly important if the problem they are facing concerns a personnel issue. It is not reasonable for the committee to expect you to come in and handle long-standing personnel problems that they could and should handle.

There is no need for you to spend your 'honeymoon' as the new pastor dealing with problems that can sabotage your time as leader of the church.

Make it a point not to be overly demanding as it relates to your salary and benefits. The committee should clearly present their plans for your provision and it is always in good taste not to suggest they offer more. Presumably, they have asked what you are currently making and will use that as a reference point in preparing your salary and benefits package.

Your wife should always accompany you for the interview so that they understand you are a unified team. Tell them about your family—their strengths and challenges, especially if there are health concerns for any of you. Let them know that your family is a top priority as you see a strong family witness as part of your responsibility.

Lastly, remember that you are interviewing them as much as they are interviewing you. You should ask them questions just as they are you. If you don't sense their wholehearted receptivity or detect resistance during your visits with the committee, it is likely you will encounter more and stronger difficulties should you accept the position. Remember, they're supposed to be on their best behavior as well!

Transparency between both parties is always the best approach. Be open and honest and as relaxed as possible. If you have a vision for the church and your role in it, share it with them. They want to know what you have in mind for what is still their church, but reassure them you would make any changes slowly, always allowing for time to develop a strong and trusting relationship with the church family.

3

So You Have a New Position

When you receive a call to serve in a new church, your first impression upon the people there is vitally important. How you relate to the staff, your peers, the deacon body, and the members-at-large during those first few days and weeks are crucial because it can set the tone and determine your effectiveness for the length of your tenure there.

In his book, "The Making of a Preacher," W. W. Melton writes: "When a minister goes to a new field, the impression he makes on the community within the first few weeks will determine in a large way his success there. If he begins to make radical changes in leadership and policies, he will soon run into difficulties." [82]

Many ministers attempt to arrive on the scene and 'fix' everything quickly before moving on to their agenda for the church. This is never a good idea. It takes time to develop relationships with the existing staff and members and to get an accurate reading on what really needs to be changed and what doesn't. I suggest waiting a full year before implementing any significant changes. Use the first year to pour into the lives of the people of the church—getting to know them well and allowing them to get to know you well. Get acquainted with their practices and their patterns of worship and ministry. Even if you know of a better or different way to do it, they will not trust you to make substantive changes in your first few months with them.

As you concentrate on these relationships in your early days, make a list of the key leaders. Go to their homes to visit and share your heart with them. By being in their home, they will be more relaxed than if you visited in a more formal setting. Let them know that you desire, above all else, to please the Lord and to bless them and the church. In getting to know you better, they will more readily trust you fully.

If you have a staff, use the first few months getting to know them as well. By developing these relationships from the start you have within you the opportunity for them to become your strongest allies or your most disappointing critics. If you don't have their respect, you will have problems in the future. I recently met with a young pastor who was forced out of his church by two staff members who demanded he be terminated. Unfortunately, most of the problems within a church are staff-related. Spend time with your staff from the start and do all that you can to make sure they support you fully.

I know of far too many pastors who failed to develop these relationships in the early days and ended up being terminated because of it. Remember, those already active in the church you are coming to have seen ministers come and go through the years. Who they impart their trust to is important because they will have to live with the programs and policies you put into place long after you're gone.

When I became pastor at First Baptist, Euless, it was after I had been an associate pastor at First Baptist, Dallas.

Many thought I had come from such a large church to Euless only as a stopover until something larger opened up. I had to put in lots of time that first year to reassure many members and church leaders that I had no intention of leaving anytime soon 'for greener pastures.'

That first year I took time to visit every ordained deacon in the church, some 125 men. I visited both the active and inactive deacons and told them I loved them, that I wanted to be their pastor, and that I would do my best to minister to them and to lead the church to the best of my abilities. After I completed these visits, I called a meeting of them all and again, shared my heart, specifically for their church. I told them I had not come for a short time and that I planned to stay for a very long time. They responded in a strong and appreciative manner, thankful for commitment to stay. In the end, we had 16 remarkable years together and experienced tremendous growth.

The key to effectiveness in accepting a position at a new church is to do so with an emphasis on developing strong relationships and trust among your people. The logistical and operational changes can wait; the relationships can't.

3 How to Leave a Church

There can be many reasons to leave your position within a church, and they all should be done with respect for the people and church you are leaving. Whether you are called to another church, retiring, or even being terminated, there are guidelines that allow everyone to maintain honor and integrity if followed.

The first and foremost practice is to never do anything to injure the church you are leaving. Regardless of the circumstances, it is never right to create problems on your way out the door. Leave graciously and gratefully for having had the opportunity to serve there; anything less than this speaks far more ill of you than anyone else. Emotions can run high during these times for all parties involved. Don't fuel the feelings by reacting to negative comments or trying to correct misplaced criticism.

When you concentrate on thanking the Lord for the privilege of serving at the church, you will be able to leave with your head held high and won't give anyone around you a reason to believe you were mistreated or angry. God is still sovereign in the middle of your departure and He will provide for you and your family. He will honor your integrity for leaving appropriately and positively.

When you leave, take the time to find a way to thank those at the church who helped you in your ministry there. Write a note of appreciation and speak positively about the church and its leadership whenever possible. If you can't find positive remarks as you leave, it is best to not comment at all. Your silence will speak sufficiently and is better than disgruntled parting shots. Maintain your honor to the Lord and be gracious until the end.

If you are retiring, there are a few more details to consider. It is usually hard for a retiring pastor to remain in the church, at least in the short-term. That's not to say it can't be done, but if you are retiring from a church, stop to prayerfully consider the impact your presence would have on the incoming pastor and remaining staff. If you remain, you must realize that you are no longer responsible for the leadership and should never have a part in criticizing their methods. If you cannot accept their practices, you should go elsewhere. Even under the best of situations, it can be awkward when a retiring pastor remains within the church, so enter into such situations with caution.

I have even known of former pastors who have led the opposition against new pastors and gone so far as to help divide the church and begin a new ministry close by. This is absolutely wrong and should never occur. If you cannot or will not fully support the new leadership of the church you are retiring from, you should worship somewhere else.

I left my last church 24 years ago and am now back worshipping there. I love my pastor and have gone to him, pledging that I will never be any kind of a problem to him and will not criticize his leadership. I am present every time I'm in town and have committed to doing anything he wants me to do. I want him to know I support him fully and completely.

Guard Your Tongue...and Pen... and Email

3

Remember when you speak a work, mail a letter, or hit 'send' on an email, it can never be retrieved. Before you speak, write, or compose, temper your tongue and consider the weight and tone of your words. Never send a letter or an email you would be ashamed of if it was shared. If it can be shared, it likely will. Even though there is no digital trail or handwritten proof, a misspoken or inappropriate word can be just as devastating. If you think before you speak or write, you won't have to worry about ill-chosen words.

The Bible has a great deal to say about the misuse of the tongue and in every instance, it encourages us to be careful in how we communicate. These are just a few of the references:

"The wise store up knowledge,
but the mouth of the fool hastens destruction."
–Proverbs 10:14

"Even a fool is considered wise when he keeps silent, discerning when he seals his lips."
–Proverbs 17:28

"A fool's mouth is his devastation,
and his lips are a trap for him."
–Proverbs 18:7

"Now when we put bits into the mouths of horses to make them obey us, we also guide the whole animal. And consider ships: Though very large and driven by fierce winds, they are guided by a very small rudder wherever the will of the pilot directs. So too, though the tongue is a small part of the body, it boasts great things. Consider how large a forest a small fire ignites. And the tongue is a fire. The tongue, a world of unrighteousness, is placed among the parts of our bodies. It pollutes the whole body, sets the course of life on fire, and is set on fire by hell." –James 3:3-6

You never have to apologize for something you almost said. Think carefully about every word you speak, write, or type. And regarding all your social media postings, remember that anything you post is available to anyone, anywhere, forever. If in doubt about what to say or how to say it, take a break from the issue. Never respond with a mind clouded by anger or frustration; the feelings will subside, but the words can live on. Err on the cautious side and carefully guard every communication you make.

Always Accept Resignations

3

If someone presents you with a resignation, always accept it. If you have to beg or persuade someone to work with you, it is wasted effort to try and change their mind. If people succeed in getting what they want by threatening their resignations, they can never be trusted from that point on to do the work of the ministry.

I once had a facility manager who also held other roles within the church. He was a deacon, chairman of the finance committee and chairman of the search committee that brought me to the church. And he lived just two houses down from me! In addition to his many church responsibilities, he was also employed full-time outside the church. I still don't know how he found the time to do it all. He was of tremendous value to the church and was by far the most admired and respected man in the church.

Whenever he tended to some repair or took care of some maintenance issue, he was always quick to say, "Now, I don't want a lot of attention—I just like working in the background." That one statement should have been a major clue, one I've since come to recognize since then—if someone tells you they don't want any special attention or recognition, they probably do want to be recognized and praised!

In my first year as pastor there, we had a deacon and wives' retreat at a nearby state encampment. One evening at the retreat I took some time to talk about our ministerial staff—to brag on them and share my appreciation for them. As I was only speaking of our ministerial staff and not the support staff (especially the part-time staff), it didn't occur to me to speak of the facilities manager.

After the session that night, he came to me and told me he was angry and disappointed that I hadn't mentioned him at all and had plans to resign. I did my best to encourage him not to resign and to express my sincere gratitude for all he did for the church as well as our personal friendship. Nothing would console him and he assured me his resignation would be on my desk Monday morning. Again, I asked that he not resign, and cautioned him not to offer his letter, as I would accept it and his employment with the church would end.

True to his word, the letter was on my desk Monday morning and true to my word, I presented it at the Wednesday evening service. I could see him standing in the back of the auditorium as I read the letter, waiting to see what would happen next. When I finished, one deacon moved to accept the letter, another one seconded the motion, and just like that, his resignation was accepted.

It grieved me to see a misunderstanding end in such a hurtful way, but I also learned a lot from this experience. Never cave to the threat of a resignation; if a person makes such a threat, he has ceased to have the heart for the ministry as their first love. Allow them the opportunity to separate from the ministry and learn to serve elsewhere.

Be Generous with Departing Co-Workers

3

God will honor your efforts when you treat departing employees and staff with abundant generosity. When you make the effort to make their departure an opportunity for love and appreciation, they will leave with fond memories of their days spent there in ministry. I always gave a reception and made available a love offering whenever staff left the church because I found it best to err on the side of graciousness and generosity.

Even when the circumstances are out of the ordinary and the reasons for the departure are unusual, I have seen God honor the actions of those who are gracious and generous even when they didn't have to be. One such incident occurred many years ago when my church brought an outstanding young man on staff as our Minister of Youth. He made the biggest impression on me of anyone I had ever served with. He was diligent, disciplined, loved working with our youth, and kept a detailed journal of his spiritual pilgrimage. He was a stellar example of a young man wholeheartedly answering his call to the Lord.

He had only been at the church a little over a month before I started hearing reports of bizarre behavior. The reports began to reveal some deep, deep problems with this young man. His issues came to a peak one Sunday morning when I was out of town. Before the morning services, the young man approached our Minister of Music and told him that God had spoken to him and that he was supposed to sing during services that day. When our Minister of Music told him that was not possible, the young man went back to the sound booth area and fell on the floor in the fetal position, totally unresponsive to any kind of communication.

He was taken to a nearby hospital where he was diagnosed as bipolar and subject to manic/depressive mood swings, a condition he didn't even realize he had. It was a shock to us all but his actions made it necessary to terminate him. Even though he had only been with us just 60 days at the time of his diagnosis, we paid for his treatment and his salary for one year.

The Lord move in the treatment process and, in time, he was restored and able to continue in ministry for many years afterward. For many years after his treatment, I received a letter from him around the anniversary of his collapse, thanking me and the church for standing by him, providing for him, and our contribution towards saving his marriage and ministry.

I have seen many people leave the churches I've pastored and during my time at LifeWay, but I've always made it a priority to treat their departure with respect, kindness and generosity. In my 15 years at LifeWay, many people left for one reason or another, and we always made a special effort to treat them with grace and generosity.

Learn from Your Failures

3

World-class surfers wipe out 90% of the time trying to catch the biggest wave. Those are staggering odds against success, but it's also the only way they'll ever learn to ride the really big waves. Sometimes those same odds face us in ministry, and like the surfers, it is only through these overwhelming times that we gain insight, experience, and maturity.

It's a given that not everything you plan will work out the way you expect. Sometimes, they won't even work out at all! Learn why they failed, what to do different or better or not at all, and move on. Don't stop reaching out and moving forward just because something didn't work; let it empower you to keep going. The biggest lessons in life usually come from failure, not success. Failure is just one way something didn't work, not the end of the effort.

I like the way William Mitchell speaks of fear in "Winning in the Land of Giants:" "Fear is rarely focused, which is part of its nature. Fear is rooted in 'I don't know' and 'I don't understand' far more than in 'I know' or 'I believe.' Sometimes the fear is a fear of failure. It may be a fear of embarrassment or a fear of loss. The most debilitating thing about this type of fear is that it prevents us from reaching out for things we might be able to achieve. This type of fear paralyzes." [83]

When I was serving at Red Bridge Baptist Church in Kansas City we had only five acres of land and one very small building. We added another small building with a full basement to help with the crowding, but as we grew, we needed to find still other ways to accommodate our congregation. We had to get creative and decided the best way was to use our buildings twice on Sunday mornings.

In preparation for this new practice, we met and planned and prayed and ultimately decided to have two Sunday School meeting times and two worship services, both with back-to-back meeting times. We didn't know of any other church at the time that was doing such a thing, so this was all unchartered territory for us. Ultimately, the split times just did not work well for our church. Some departments remained overcrowded while the others dwindled to only two or three members. It wasn't an efficient or effective use of our resources to hold two separate meeting times.

We didn't quit, though, in our determination to better serve our growing membership. Just because the first attempt didn't work, didn't mean there wasn't another suitable way to meet our challenging growth. We tried a new schedule: we asked all the adults who were not serving or teaching during the Bible study hour to come to one service and then students and workers in grades 4 through high school come to the second service. It worked wondrously!

It was a bit demanding on me because it meant I would be preaching two different messages—one primarily to adults and one to children, youth and their workers—but it was worth the extra effort. In our small facility that was originally stretched to house only 300 people, we were able to average over 500 people in attendance by dividing our services this way. We all learned from what didn't work and went on to figure out what did work!

Another time at this same church, I began to show Billy Graham movies on a big bed sheet stretched across part of the parking lot. I touted it as a 'drive-in' type movie theater. It wasn't a rousing success, but it did help our staff think outside the box and to focus on ways to reach our community in a more effective way.

Don't allow the fear of failure to deter you from trying new things. Failures are wonderful opportunities to learn from and to gain insight into what really does work. You will always learn more from trying and failing than from your successes. God uses failure as a means of drawing us closer to Him. Every day, we miss the opportunity for divine encounters to draw closer to Him when we become sidelined by our failures.

Erwin McManus presents a great perspective on this in his book, "Seizing Your Divine Moment." He says, "We fail to see divine moments when all we see is danger and risk of failure. We lose our confidence in the midst of divine moments when the journey becomes turbulent and God allows us to experience failure." [84] Our failures are just as divinely orchestrated as our successes are; don't lose sight of this fact and allow God to strengthen you through the trials and errors of growth.

Continually Stretch Yourself—Raise the Bar!

In all of life, never settle for mediocrity. Don't allow complacency to take the place of excellence or be content with offering less than your best efforts. Discipline must be present in every area of your life—especially your ministry. Because the ministry is one of the few vocations that does not require you to perpetually update your skills and education, you have to be proactive in the refining process.

Think about other practicing professionals—teachers have to pursue continuing education credits to remain in the classroom; doctors and medical professionals must always remain attuned to emerging treatments and best practices; lawyers have to stay constantly abreast of changing laws and judicial interpretations. Preachers don't have any mandatory guidelines for remaining in service yet relevancy is crucial for our message to be received. Preaching methods and presentation practices must also be continually refined. We must be learning even as we are teaching.

Proverbs challenges us to always remain teachable as a lifetime learner. These words sound the call to always learn:

"My son, if you accept my words
and store up my commands within you,
listening closely to wisdom
and directing your heart to understanding;
furthermore, if you call out to insight
and lift your voice to understanding,
if you seek it like silver,
and search for it like hidden treasure,
then you will understand the fear of the Lord
and discover the knowledge of God."

—Proverbs 2:1-5

In another one of his books, "Uprising, Revolution of the Soul," Erwin McManus also addresses the intense need for wisdom and growing in God: "The life that God calls you to cannot be lived without wisdom. I am thankful that God calls people like me, who have lived foolishly, to follow Him. But the journey cannot be engaged if we choose to remain the fool." [85] The Lord makes wisdom available to all of us in a moment-by-moment fashion. It is there for the taking and for the foolish to ignore.

For years, the Fort Worth Star-Telegram ran a column by popular humorist George Dolan. He often wrote about the exploits of a West Texas Baptist deacon named Bev King. Bev owned the bank and a good part of the town of Graham, Texas. He had a huge ranch and investments in many other areas yet chose to spend his days on the courthouse square, sitting and whittling with some of the town's retired gentlemen.

One day, a young traveling salesman came to town and pulled up in front of the town's lone hotel, just across from where the men sat. When he got out of his car, he couldn't hide his contempt for the small town including the lack of a bellman for help with his suitcases. He saw the men and called out for some help, offering to tip them for their effort.

Bev offered to help and began carrying the young man's suitcases up the steps of the old hotel. As the man was offering the tip, he said, "I saw the most beautiful ranch house I have ever seen just outside of Graham with wild animals around it like a zoo and a beautiful lake and impressive grounds like nothing else in West Texas—who does that belong to?"

In a droll response, Bev replied, "It belongs to me." "How in the world did you get that ranch?" the salesman asked smugly.

"Carried my own bags," said Bev.

When it comes to being a lifetime learner, we must learn to carry our own bags and be responsible for maintaining a disciplined approach to learning and bettering ourselves.

As ministers, we need to approach our ministry with the same kind of discipline as those in the secular world. Just as society is forever changing and developing, we also need to be sharpening our ministry skills to better affect culture. Believe me when I say that the challenges of preaching today are incredibly different than they were 60 years ago when I first started.

As a young pastor, I lived in a world where schools and other organizations would not schedule anything on Sundays (all day!) or Wednesday nights because those times were recognized as special for the church. Few businesses even opened on Sundays. The minister was the most respected member of the community and the church was the center of activity for most citizens. When a family relocated to a new town, their first order of business, after finding a home, was to connect with a church. It was usually good for business for a man to be active in his church.

Much of this has changed now. The church is no longer the center of most communities nor is the minister any longer the most respected member of the community. In fact, he is oftentimes way down on the list of most respected citizens. Schools, communities, sports organizations, and more now regularly plan activities, games, performances, and the like on Sundays—even Sunday mornings. Wednesday evenings have long since been absorbed into the other activities of families. This is clearly not the church of our fathers and grandfathers.

Yet still, in the middle of these huge cultural changes, we are still to remain steadfast in our refusal to settle into mediocrity or neglect to improve our understanding of our roles and new opportunities as they present themselves. Times have changed, but our call to effective ministry has not. Methods and practices to reach the lost have undergone a tremendous transformation, but the message remains unchanged. We are called to always seek to improve our presentation of God's Word by whatever communication is most effective for the days and times. And whether it is through text or tweet, on the street corners or in the church, our most important resource is God's anointing on the ministry He has given us and that will never change.

3

Prepare for the Unexpected

It is important to have a schedule, but not to be a slave to it. One of the first lessons we learn as ministers is that there is a vast difference between the urgent and the important. As I've mentioned before, urgent things are not always important and important things are often not urgent. If we are slaves to our schedule, we run the risk of missing out on some of God's greatest interruptions for our lives. Plan well, but always be prepared to change as situations arise.

The first time I went to Kenya, I thought I would be preaching revival services at First Baptist Church of Mombasa, Kenya. I did do that, but Sunday services were just the beginning. The rest of the time we were out in the streets, at the crossroads and meeting places of the city, or sharing the Gospel from the back of a pick-up truck.

We worked in teams throughout our days there. Some of us would give the Gospel presentation for about five minutes and then extend the invitation. Of the many that would respond every time, one of us would take a group of them to a different area to counsel with them, confirm their decisions, get their information for following up, and give them printed materials to take with them. While one team was carrying out the counseling details, another would begin sharing the Gospel again and start the whole process over.

Over the course of two weeks, we watched thousands of people come to put their faith in Christ. The way it happened, however, was not at all what we expected. It was our job to be flexible and adapt to the opportunities before us, not overlook them. I had planned to preach one way, but God had a different and better plan.

In ministry, much of what you plan and plan for may never happen. Or it might happen, but not in the time frame you expect or not in the manner you anticipate. You will spend a great deal of your time in the ministry changing plans and strategies and adapting to frequently changing circumstances and conditions. Don't allow this to shut you down and discourage you. Always be ready to adapt to the current challenge and make adjustments to try something a different way. Flexibility is a requirement for ministry. If a strategy doesn't work well one way, move on and try another way…or another strategy. When you prepare for the unexpected you are better able to overcome obstacles and challenges. You know there will always be circumstances you can't fully control, but you can always control how you respond to them.

3

Evaluate Your Strategy

There is one question you must always ask yourself whenever starting a new ministry, outreach effort, building fund, or any other project as it relates to your ministry. And that question is:

"How is what I am doing bringing glory to God and promoting His Kingdom?"

If we can answer this, then we can explain why we do what we do in the way that we do it. If we can answer this, we can be confident we are seeking God's favor. If we can answer this, we can save ourselves and our churches much wasted effort from tending to unnecessary tasks and pursuing goals that honor man more than God.

If we can answer this, the revival would be unimaginable.

At LifeWay, I had a plaque put on every desk that read, "How is what I am doing helping the churches?" It was important to me that our staff keep 'the main thing the main thing' and not lose sight of their personal ministry in dealing with the churches. It was a quiet reminder that made a big impact.

To answer either of these important questions properly, it requires us to continually evaluate what we are doing, why we are doing it, and how we can do it better. If we're always cognizant of the how and why of what we're doing, we will be better motivated to do a job honorable to Christ.

Businesses apply the bell curve to evaluate the how's and why's of what they do to increase their efficiency. It is based on the principle that everything they do will increase maximum effectiveness to a point and then begin declining. If we apply this theory to ministry, we want to be ready to change whenever what we're doing is at the top of the curve and not wait until effectiveness starts to decline. If we continually evaluate our programs and activities, how we spend our time and our resources, and where we place our priorities, we can protect against being caught in the downturn of effectiveness.

One of the real challenges in determining how to use a church's limited resources is to decide whether or not something done in the past is a valuable tool for the future. Everything that has been useful in the past is not necessarily helpful in the present, and certainly not always so for the future. Nothing should be cast away just because we have done it before, and no idea should be eliminated for no other reason than it has never been done before.

Many times our ministries get caught up in doing something because that's the way it was when we arrived or it is just a long-standing practice of the church. Budgets are particularly susceptible to this practice because usually we plan a future budget based on what we spent the previous year. We rarely ask ourselves, "Is this worth doing again?" and more frequently assume if we did something last year, we should do it again this year. When we approve budgets and programs without careful evaluation, we never stop to fully determine the real value of what we are doing and its part in reaching our goals. This results in our goals never being properly evaluated and never being able to assess future plans for their value and effectiveness.

I have found it helpful to get benchmarks from other, comparable ministries to see how their plans measure up in comparison. In seeing what other churches of similar size and demographics do and how they reach their goals, it helps you evaluate your programs. Just be mindful not to compare your ministry to much larger or different kinds of ministry as so many of the key variables are not the same—number of members and/or volunteers, size of budget, mission emphasis, etc. Learn from what these larger institutions do and see if it applies it to your ministry.

One of the best ways I know of to encourage every program and practice to stand on its own is to start every year with a clean slate—a totally clean slate. For budgeting, this means you begin with a zero-based budget, one that can only be developed by accurate appraisals of every activity included in the budget. The same principle applies to planning activities. Just because something has been done one way, doesn't mean it should continue to be done that way. Likewise, just because something is new doesn't mean it is suddenly the right way to do something and shouldn't be evaluated alongside existing projects.

Whether you're reviewing projects, programs, budgets, or priorities for a department within a church or the church as a whole, allow each decision you make concerning church resources to be based on a careful review and evaluation. When you make the call as to how it pertains to furthering the Gospel or furthering Kingdom strategies, the decisions become considerably easier to make.

Don't Quit Before You Finish

Don't Quit
Before You **FINISH**

4

This is God's Ministry!

4

Be Ambitious for God's Kingdom

Great leaders in any enterprise are noted first for their great passion and ambition for their companies; not for themselves. God created the church in the first place as an instrument for His Glory and the mission has not changed since. Paul passionately preached on behalf of Christ's glory when he spoke to the Ephesians saying,

"Now to Him who is able to do above and beyond all that we ask or think according to the power that works in us—to Him be the glory in the church and in Christ Jesus to all generations, forever and ever. Amen." –Ephesians 3:20-21

Just as I spoke of evaluating every program and activity of the church against the scrutiny of thoughtful questions, we should also ask certain questions of ourselves. If we are passionate about living and serving in a way that brings glory to God, we will always temper all that we do and say in response to this:

"How is what I am doing bringing glory to God and enhancing His Kingdom?"

How we answer this question as it pertains to the present and the future says a lot about our vision for The Kingdom. Great leaders set up their ministries for even greater success in the future. Alfred North Whitehead captured the essence of this when he said, "A wise man is a man who plants shade trees he will never sit under." [87] This is the spirit that should permeate every ministry at every church. We are not here for ourselves or even our generation. We are here for future generations.

Jesus knew this and practiced this with His disciples. He deliberately told them:

"I assure you: The one who believes in Me will also do the works that I do. And he will do even greater works than these, because I am going to the Father." –John 14:12

Jesus set up His followers to do better than He did and to do more than He did and He rejoiced in it! Jesus confined His ministry to the boundaries of Israel, a country no bigger than the state of Vermont, but he intended for His disciples to go well beyond the borders. And well they did.

- Jesus never went to Athens or preached in Rome; Paul did.

- Jesus never preached in Jerusalem, bringing 3,000 new believers to the Faith; Peter did.

- Jesus never preached in Antioch resulting in thousands of Romans cheering on Him and His message; Chrysostom did.

- Jesus never preached to a crowd of 5,000 into His fourth decade in London; Spurgeon did.

Though these are just a few of the examples of men who came after Jesus, all of them went further, shared more, and converted more souls to believers than Christ did…and that just the way He planned it. Jesus' attitude was that He was laying the foundation for those who would come after him to reach farther and wider in their influence for The Kingdom.

Like Jesus, our ministry is not about us. It is not about our gifts, our creativity, or our skills. It's not about anything that is anything about us. God has called us to be instruments for His glory. We are to communicate the Gospel to a lost world and we are to be ambitious in our reach for God's Kingdom.

4 Demonstrate Humility

Humility is at the heart of character, consistency, and compassion. However large a role you play in a project or activity, be sure to shine the spotlight of success on others who were a part of it. Allow others to receive the credit for success because you will never succeed unless those you work with succeed also. If you always seek the credit when things go right, you must also accept the blame when things go wrong. Don't make the mistake of hogging the credit; it can be a deadly trap!

It is your job to bring out the best in your team and inspire them to do exceptional things. Humility on your part will always inspire people more than arrogance. Remember, we are all standing on the shoulders of others, and true success comes from building a team spirit of unity of purpose.

When we act in humility, we find the real purpose of life. We come to God with simple faith, acknowledging our sinfulness and our failures. Turning to Jesus Christ and accepting His gift of salvation is the greatest act of humility we can do and brings us the greatest fulfillment in life. That is why unselfish service is at the heart of ministry. We can honor God in no greater way than to serve in humility.

In "The Book of Leadership," John MacArthur said, "Paul said he was the chief of sinners (I Timothy 1:15). As far as he was concerned, his own merits were worthless. He counted them as dung, excrements, the lowest kind of filth (Philemon 3:8). If it weren't for the priceless treasure God had entrusted to him, he would have no value at all. That is true humility, and it is one of the keys to Paul's effectiveness as a leader." [86]

The way to lasting greatness is the way of humility; the way of Jesus Christ, not the way of Lucifer. For believers, the words of Satan are hard to even tolerate, but show his incredible arrogance towards Christ:

" You said to yourself:
'I will ascend to the heavens;
I will set up my throne
above the stars of God.
I will sit on the mount of the gods' assembly,
in the remotest parts of the North.

I will ascend above the highest clouds;
I will make myself like the Most High.'"

–Isaiah 14:13-14

Diotrephes, "who loves to have first place..." (3 John 9) clearly followed the path of Satan and placed his honor above Christ's—the complete opposite of how we are called to be. God calls us to be shepherds of His sheep as humble leaders, not as arrogant CEOs, drill sergeants, dictators, or spiritual superstars.

If we stop to ask ourselves several key questions, we can become more focused and will therefore have a greater opportunity to serve as Christ in our ministry. Before you get too far down the path of your ministry and become consumed with the details of programs and growth patterns, stop to ask yourself these questions:

- What is the measure of true ministerial greatness?

- What is the signature or the abiding truth of a truly great minister, one that is great in the eternal gaze of God's eyes and not just the temporal assessment of man's myopia?

- How can we, as ministers, run our race and finish our course so that, at the end of day, we will know we were true to the Master's intent for ministry?

If we consider the example set by the life and career of a man widely considered one of the greatest ministers of all time, London pastor Charles Spurgeon, we can learn a tremendous amount. Hailed by such spiritual giants as German pastor Helmut Thielecke and American Independent Baptist leader John R. Rice, Spurgeon is frequently regarded as the greatest of the greats. But what exactly was the essence of his greatness?

Shortly after his death at 56, the first of many biographers attempted to capture the mystery of his remarkable and storied life. The author chose what he considered to be Spurgeon's greatest moment and surprisingly, it wasn't any of the usual hallmarks we traditionally associate with a life of accomplishment. In his career, Spurgeon did tremendous things, including:

- attracting the largest indoors crowd ever-to-date gathered to hear someone preach;

- the building of the enormous Metropolitan Tabernacle which he filled morning and night into his fourth decade;

- the founding of Spurgeon's College to train and equip ministers;

- departing from the British Baptist Union in the Downgrade Controversy.

What this particular biographer considered the greatest moment of Spurgeon's accomplished life of ministry occurred as a 12-year-old orphan boy lay dying at Spurgeon's Stockwell Orphanage. Years before, Spurgeon had founded the orphanage to care for the street children of Dickens' London. Hundreds of children owed their very lives to him. As a frequent visitor to the orphanage, Spurgeon was always greeted by the cheers and hugs of the children he helped save.

On one such occasion, a nurse asked him to visit a dying boy in the infirmary. The young boy was dying of consumption, or what we've come to know as tuberculosis. Spurgeon asked the boy, "Laddie, are you ready to meet the Savior?"

The little boy assured the great pastor of his salvation and readiness to be in Christ's presence. And then, Spurgeon asked if there was anything the boy wanted.

"I always wanted a bird in a cage," the boy replied.

It was a simple enough request, but one Spurgeon took to heart immediately. He called for his horse-drawn carriage and quickly began racing from shop to shop, hoping to secure a bird in a cage. When at last he located and purchased a bird in a cage, Spurgeon raced back to the orphanage, intent on fulfilling the boy's final request.

He made it just in time, beating death's shadow by only moments. In doing so, Spurgeon was possibly at his most Christ-like—caring deeply, purposefully, and personally for an unknown street urchin in need. It's no wonder the biographer selected this as his finest moment.

It is of no consequence that 56 volumes of his sermons are still in print and available today electronically. Nor is it significant that he is still quoted from and credited with inspiring sermons the world over. The notoriety was not his goal nor his greatest achievement; that came in his quiet servanthood that few ever knew about except a handful of orphanage workers and a dying young boy.

Like Spurgeon, when we exhibit a character of humility, we inspire others to be and do their best. This is the mark of genuine ministry.

Early in His ministry, the Lord Jesus faced three major temptations to use His own greater power for His own immediate enrichment, ease, and comfort. These are chronicled in the Books of Matthew and Luke. The first temptation was to turn stones to bread to satisfy His hunger. There before Him, He was challenged to use His extraordinary powers as the Messiah to turn the stones of the Judean desert into loaves of bread. He could literally speak the stones into bread and end His hunger immediately, but there was so much more at risk than His personal hunger.

Beyond the hunger pangs rested what could have been a one-way ticket to glory, wealth, and fame. That's because, in a world where the majority of people went to bed hungry every night, He could have been declared the bread-messiah. He would have been hailed as the greatest of all men ever to live, and could have led the ravenously hungry mob of Judeans in the revolution of His choosing.

Instead, Jesus refused to use His God-give powers for His own personal satisfaction. He knew there was a greater cause at hand—the Kingdom of God—and that obedience to it required the subjection of His own ego to the larger purpose of His coming. He had the wisdom and foresight to understand that the foundation of the Kingdom of God and the subsequent redemption of humanity were resting on the actions He took. He knew, despite His hunger, that to fill His own belly with bread made from stones would have made Him a traitor to His greater mission.

The second temptation was to leap off the pinnacle of the Temple to demonstrate the intense promise of protection He was given as God's Son. Because the rabbis had taught that the Messiah would appear at the top of the Temple, it would have made quite the show for Jesus to stand at the top and float slowly to the ground 1,000 feet below. It would have been the publicity stunt to end all publicity stunts and would have silenced the zealots gathered below that were fighting to end the Roman regime. Instead, Jesus refused to take the cheap, quick leap to personal power and chose the long and painful march to the Cross to build something that would last infinitely longer than any ruling class or empire.

Lastly, the third temptation that faced Christ was the offer to bow down to Satan and be granted all power over the entire earth. That's a heady offer—immediate gratification and consummate power. I imagine the offer must have looked somewhat plausible as He stood on the highest mountaintop in the world. Looking out, He could see the Roman triremes splitting the waters of the Mediterranean Sea, embodying the power that could have been His. In a single gesture, He could have used His powers to unseat any Roman emperor throughout the entire empire. And for all this, He need only kneel before Satan. But He refused.

Jesus wanted to invest in the eternal—not temporary governments of men, not the easily satisfied grumblings of His stomach, not the fickle attention of self-centered men. He wanted His efforts to last. So instead of dining with the members of the Roman ruling class and other members of the elite society, Jesus chose to pour His life into the most despised and powerless men in society, those without the trappings of success to weigh them down.

Out of these men Christ built a following that would last forever. The humble figure of our Lord Jesus Christ tells us that the only way to save our life is to sacrifice it to a larger cause—His larger cause. Christ's pattern of humility and strength controlled by the Holy Spirit should be the goal of every minister.

If Christ, as the Son of God and co-creator of the cosmic universe, did not think equality with God was something to be grasped, then surely we shouldn't entertain the consideration either. In fact, for all His powers and omniscience, Christ intentionally acted contrary to all the resources at His disposal. Here is Paul's testament to the character of Christ to the Philippians:

"Make your own attitude that of Christ Jesus,
who, existing in the form of God,
did not consider equality with God
as something to be used for His own advantage.
Instead He emptied Himself
by assuming the form of a slave,
taking on the likeness of men
And when He had come as a man
in His external form,
He humbled Himself by becoming obedient
to the point of death—
even to death on a cross."

–Philippians 2:5-8

Time after time, Christ made Himself of no reputation and humbled Himself before others. He came from the glory of the throne of God to the obscurity of a cow stable in Bethlehem. And yet, some 2,000+ years later, the grandest cause for celebration on the planet turns its attention toward this humble place every December. The entire planet does not turn its eyes towards the marble halls of Caesar's Rome at Christmas time. Men do not think about the Parthenon and Mars Hill of Athens at Christmas. Every year much of the world's population turns its hearts and eyes toward a lowly stable that first housed the Son of God.

What more evidence should we need that humble intensity is the way to lasting leadership? Can we name a single moment when Jesus exercised His prerogatives and called attention to Himself over the Father and His Kingdom? Emphatically, we cannot! Christ always chose to honor God above all else. Hear His words to the rich, young ruler who came to Him with words of flattery: "'Why do you ask Me about what is good?' He said to him. 'There is only One who is good...'"(Matthew 19:17).

Jesus always provided the example we are to follow as ministers of the Gospel of Christ. Whenever He had the opportunity to aggrandize himself or posture Himself in a godlike stance, He deflected the attention from Himself and onto the Father.

Jesus' disciples also acted consistently with His example. When Barnabas and Paul were hailed as Zeus and Hermes while traveling through Lystra, they were quick to correct the misunderstanding. Though they had healed a man crippled from birth and the priest made efforts to sacrifice to them as gods, Paul would have nothing to do with the honor. His response for the ages tells the story: "'Men! Why are you doing these things? We are men also, with the same nature as you,...'" (Acts 14:15). At the moment they could have claimed divinity and presented themselves as gods, these two obedient disciples claimed otherwise and took their rightful place besides their fellow, fallible mankind.

There are no super heroes among Christ's followers. The best of the best of us can come no nearer to God than the worst of the worst. We all come through the shed blood of Jesus Christ. This is the great equalizer among men and as such, we should all be humbled.

4 Communicate the Vision

You have to know where you're going before you can begin to make progress towards that end. So do all of your members. Once you cast a vision for serving Christ and meeting the needs of your community and beyond, those who follow you can see the way to a preferred future. They can see the role they play in fulfilling the vision and become engaged in the project. Whatever the project or mission or outreach program, your people will need information and inspiration to support the vision.

George Barna provides a powerful definition of vision in his book, "The Power of Vision:" "Vision is a picture held in your mind's eye of the way things could or should be in the days ahead. Vision connotes a visual reality, a portrait of conditions that do not exist currently." [87] It is your job to keep your people's eye focused on the future and not on the past. To do so, you must provide a vision for them. Prayerfully beseech the Father to instill in you a vision for what He wants to do through your church and ministry.

In his book, "Leading Change," John Kotter lays out the purposes of an effective vision: "Vision refers to a picture of the future with some implicit or explicit commentary on why people should strive to create that future. In a change process, a good vision serves three important purposes. First, by clarifying the general direction for change. Second, it motivates people to take action in the right direction, even if the initial steps are personally painful. Third, it helps coordinate the actions of different people in a remarkably fast and efficient way." [88]

Take stock of your community, your facilities, and your membership with an eye towards the unmet needs in each of these areas. It is vital for churches to enrich the lives of those in their own community. Make it a priority to address the needs of those closest to you before setting out to reach places far away. Even though the prevailing (and growing!) attitude and belief of the current leadership of our country is that the government should take care of all the needs of the people, this is a recipe for a disaster whose day is soon coming. There has yet to be an example of success when this approach is taken.

The fault in this practice is plain and obvious: the government cannot possibly do anything for anyone without first taking something from someone else to do it. As the government has no funds of its own and produces no real product, the only funds it maintains come from its citizens. Government can, and continues to do so increasingly, distribute what it takes from one citizen to another, but it cannot originate these funds and products on its own. It is a perpetually ill-fated example of "robbing from Peter to pay Paul."

The church, however, has shown time and time again that it can build a strategy to serve its home community. Through voluntary giving, not mandatory taxation, the church can immediately affect those nearby, meeting their short-term needs and empowering them to address their long-term needs.

As an example, the church, where I now hold membership, has a food and clothing distribution system for the most needy in our community. Additionally, we lead a network of 15-20 neighboring churches to help with home repairs for the poor and to provide backpacks and school supplies for thousands of area children. By meeting these significant needs to those closest to us, we have been given tremendous access to our surrounding school districts and communities. This has, in turn, given us great opportunities to minister to people who would not likely ever come to our church. These opportunities have led to thousands of souls coming to know the Lord in the last 10 years.

Let God give you a vision for your community to communicate with enthusiasm and conviction to your members. Then, lead the way in implementing the strategy that God has given you. Every church should make it a goal to focus on things beyond itself. In fact, the church, for all its services and programs for members, is possibly the only organized institution that exists primarily for non-members. It's the people outside our services we want to come in; not those already inside.

When given a vision for meeting the needs of our neighbors, we have to go to great lengths to make sure our people are informed and inspired in order to become engaged. This is what Pat McMillan says about the inherent responsibility of effective communication in "The Performance Factor:" "Communication appears to be deceptively easy. However, most of us carry a major misconception about the process: that communication is primarily message sending. Communication does not take place until someone receives the message and understands it as the sender intended. The most eloquent speech or the most beautifully composed letter isn't a successful communication if it misses the mark." [89]

We must remember that we are not just responsible for what we say, but for what people hear!

Be Redemptive

4

God's word gives us clear instructions about redeeming those who have fallen. In Galatians, Paul tells the people, "Brothers, if someone is caught in any wrongdoing, you who are spiritual should restore such a person with a gentle spirit, watching out for yourselves so you also won't be tempted" (Galatians 6:1). It is a fact of life that every Christian leader faces severe temptation and is under constant Satanic attack. When Satan can engineer the fall of a Christian leader or a minister of the Gospel falls into sinful habits, it is a tragic triumph for Satan because of his widespread influence.

Some of this fallout is due to us as believers. We often expect our ministers to be blameless in every way. This is not only unreasonable, it is also wrong. By placing them on a pedestal, we tempt them to entertain thoughts of special privilege. This can lead them to becoming vulnerable and naïve in their own natural abilities. Because ministers are, by nature, usually sensitive to the needs of others, they also become more vulnerable than most.

While it is impossible to expect our pastors and preachers to be completely without fault, it is not unreasonable to expect them to live a life above reproach. I Timothy speaks of this mandate: "…If anyone aspires to be an overseer, he desires a noble work. An overseer, therefore, must be above reproach,…" (I Timothy 3:1-2). Make no mistake—the man and the message are inseparably linked. Lose faith in one and you lose faith in the other. As ministers called to convey the Word of God, we are always on public display. It is incumbent upon us to display the highest integrity possible if we are to effectively represent the Gospel to a desperate and hurting world.

II Samuel tells the story of a leader who failed on a grand scale, on a grand stage. King David committed acts of immorality as well as murder. His story begins with acts of rebellion and other sins and soon escalated to complete and widespread chaos. Things went from bad to worse quickly and severely once David allowed sin to take over his heart and mind. The child born to Bathsheba died. David's own family lived in chaos, disloyalty, hate, jealousy and shame.

The truth is, it is never easy to restore faith in leaders who fall into sin—especially when it is sexual sin. That is why the trust in you that your members and those you influence have is so incredibly precious. When this trust is betrayed, the ministry is likely doomed. If there is any chance for restoration of the person or the ministry, the sin must be confronted and repentance forthcoming. This is never easy as pride and egos are involved and confrontation is uncomfortable at best.

As I mentioned in a previous section, ministers must be accountable. We are first accountable to God and then to the church. God calls us to morality, integrity, and accountability in our ministries and our churches. Each man must stand responsible for his sins. Though his sins were many, David did just that—he assumed full responsibility and gave no excuse. We should do likewise.

When we try to justify our sins or make excuses for our actions, it as though we are not trusting the grace of God to forgive our sins. It is a matter of choosing to justify ourselves or justify God. We cannot do both. If I am right then God is wrong. When I admit my full responsibility for my sins, I am also accepting that God is right.

Just as David went 'all in' in pursuing his wants versus God's desires, he also came to repentance with an 'all in' heartHear his cries of repentance in Psalms:

"Be gracious to me, God,
according to Your faithful love;
according to Your abundant compassion,

blot out my rebellion.
Wash away my guilt
and cleanse me from my sin.
For I am conscious of my rebellion,
and my sin is always before me.
Against You—You alone—I have sinned
And done this evil in Your sight..."

–Psalms 51:1-4

When you look closely at this confession, you realize that David confessed that his sin was against God. Most of us see his sin in a social context rather than as a divine betrayal. What about what he did to Uriah and Bathsheba? In sinning against them, David did something far more outrageous—he scorned and openly despised the One who declared Himself to be their God as well. For David to murder Uriah was to commit blasphemy against Uriah's God.

It was as if murder of a man was something David's conscience could accommodate, but to murder a man who belonged to God was a different story and more than he could accept. This is what Paul was speaking of when he said, "Now when you sin like this against the brothers and wound their weak conscience, you are sinning against Christ" (I Corinthians 8:12). This is the way it is for each of us today. Our sins against our fellow man are ultimately, sins against our God. We must accept the responsibility of our sinful nature before we can begin to seek forgiveness and work towards restoration with Christ. David's cry for healing and cleansing is a good place to start:

"Search me, God, and know my heart;

test me and know my concerns.

See if there is any offensive way in me;

Lead me in the everlasting way."

–Psalms 51:3-4

Imagine how closely our walk with Christ would be if we were to pray this heartfelt prayer every time we sinned. The effect would be transformative!

Several years ago one of my staff ministers faced a crisis in his ministry and his marriage. He and his wife came to me and she confessed that she had fallen into an act of immorality. No one had learned of it or caught her in the act; it was God's conviction that brought her to this point. She had confessed her sins to God, her husband, and her children, and was now coming to me to express her repentance.

I immediately told her husband that, as the head of his family, it was his job to restore the marriage and his family. I relieved him of his church-related responsibilities and the church provided several months of counseling.

Since he was a staff member, we felt it appropriate for her to come before our congregation to confess her sin and share her repentance. They agreed and the next Sunday morning I announced that I would preach that evening on how to restore a fallen Christian leader. There was no reason to suspect anything other than our usual Sunday night format as this was in the midst of the time when several nationally known Christian leaders had fallen in a very public manner. Interest in this subject was unusually high.

That night our auditorium was packed as I preached the biblical admonition to restore one who had fallen into sin from Galatians 6. At the end of the message, I asked our people, "Do you believe what I have preached tonight?" The congregation responded with a resounding "Yes!" And then, I told them that I was going to give them a chance to prove it.

I brought the staff minister and his wife to the platform and in a carefully worded and very appropriate manner, she read her confession and asked for the church's forgiveness as her husband stood beside her. When she finished, I had them kneel at the altar and asked our people to come forward and pray over them. It was an electrifying moment for all of us present. The Lord's presence was upon us all, especially the couple.

Though many years have since past, many of those present still point to that evening as one of the most significant events in our ministry. To see the faith of our people in action— forgiving and loving a fellow sinner—was a night I will never forget. Wonderfully, the end of the story is that the couple's marriage was completely restored and they remain active in a strong ministry for the Lord.

When we are redemptive in our ministries, we are given a front row seat to witnessing fallen believers become restored in Christ. This strengthens our ministries, our churches, and our impact for Christ like nothing else can.

Perception is the Cruelest Form of Reality

4

This can sometimes be one of the hardest lessons to learn as a minister. Whatever is said or believed to be true doesn't have to be true to be hurtful. All it takes is for something to be perceived to be true for it to become a reality to the one with that perception. Facts become irrelevant when perception trumps proof. It is a battle of subtleties, which causes us to go on the defensive for beliefs only assumed, not valid. It is oftentimes a losing battle and one best avoided if at all possible.

That is why the Bible is so crystal clear about avoiding the trap of misperceptions in all that we say and do. These verses bear this challenge out:

Regarding the appearance of evil –

"Stay away from every kind of evil."

–I Thessalonians 5:22

Regarding the need to be beyond reproach –

"An overseer, therefore, must be above reproach, the husband of one wife, self-controlled, sensible, respectable…(If anyone does not know how to manage his own household, how will he take care of God's church?)" –I Timothy 3:2, 5)

Regarding being an example –
"…you should be an example to the believers in speech, in conduct, in love, in faith, in purity."

–I Timothy 4:12

Regarding never allowing Satan a foothold in our lives –
"…don't give the Devil an opportunity."

–Ephesians 4:27

We can never be too careful or cautious about giving the wrong perception to others. Innocent things than seem minor to us can be used by Satan to misrepresent our intentions, words, and actions—especially in matters concerning the opposite sex. Always err on the cautious side—don't handle church funds, don't confront others without another party present, and don't allow yourself to be placed in situations where the appearance is evenly slightly questionable.

When you protect your reputation, you are protecting your family. You are protecting the calling of the ministry. And most importantly, you are protecting the efforts of those who proclaim Christ to the world.

Everyone is of Great Value

4

There are no unimportant people in God's economy—everyone is important! Go out of your way to give credit and applaud the efforts of everyone who contributes to the ministry. When people feel their contributions are of worth to the ministry, their sense of stewardship increases. Do all you can to help others feel responsible for ministry successes and help them to see it is for God's Glory, whose ministry it is. We ae stewards of the ministry God gives us.

The Apostle Paul put it this way, "A person should consider us in this way: as servants of Christ and managers of God's mysteries. In this regard, it is expected of managers that each one of them be found faithful" (I Corinthians 4:1-2).

Everyone with whom we serve has a role in God's economy and a place in His Kingdom. Paul's first letter to the Corinthians compared the work of the ministry to the different parts and uses of the body:

> "For as the body is one and has many parts, and all the parts of that body, though many, are one body—so also is Christ…But now God has placed each one of the parts in one body just as He wanted. And if they were all the same part, where would the body be? Now there are many parts, yet one body." –I Corinthians 12:12, 18-20

Just as there are no unimportant or unnecessary parts to each of our own bodies, there are also no unimportant or unnecessary members of the body of Christ. Give to each person with whom you serve the dignity and encouragement they deserve with special attention paid to their contributions to Christ's Kingdom. Take the time to praise them, challenge them, admonish and correct them when necessary, and to always remind them of their value to the ministry and to Christ.

4
Never Compromise Your Convictions

Each of us, as ministers of the Gospel, will have a theology that we believe is what the Bible teaches. We believe that the Bible guides us in what we are to believe doctrinally, how we are to relate to others, how we are to comfort and bless those we serve, and how to live with purity and integrity throughout all of our life's experiences. No matter the battles you face, the changing tide of popular belief, or shifting boundaries of societal norms, stand by these beliefs. Do not compromise the theological and ethical principles God's Word proclaims.

You don't have to be offensive in your stance, but you must be firm. You can be authoritative without being demanding. And you can be decisive while remaining gentle and wise. The strength of your convictions need not be brutal.

Even if you stand alone in your beliefs, don't concede and compromise the truth of Scripture.

For everything that is good, there is a corresponding compromise which is evil. In fact, the very essence of sin is the perversion of that which is good and pleasing to the Lord. We sin when we take or use something God intended for good and use it in ways God never intended—ways that are harmful, hurtful or perverted. Simply put, sin is the compromise of God's truth.

One of the most remarkable examples of compromise is seen in the deliverance of Israel out of Egypt. At every turn Pharaoh offered distinct compromises to the Lord's people if they would only remain. Four times he offered; four times they refused.

The first compromise Pharaoh offered was for the Israelites to remain in Egypt and to make their sacrifice there. But God had other plans. He told Moses to tell Pharaoh, " ... Let My people go, so that they may worship Me" (Exodus 8:20). Pharaoh was not to be dissuaded and replied, " ...Go sacrifice to your God within the country" (Exodus 8:25). Not only would this have been a disobedience to God, but it also would have aroused the wrath of the Egyptians when they saw the animals they worshipped being sacrificed by the Israelites. To remain in Egypt for the Israelites was a lose-lose proposition—they would anger both God and the Egyptians! Pharaoh's first pass at trying to convince the Israelites to stay was to engage them in negotiating with him. For them and for us, it has never been, nor will ever it ever be, right to compromise by negotiating God's commands.

The second compromise Pharaoh offered the people was for them to take care of their business, but to return just as if nothing had happened. When Moses told the ruler where he was to lead the people, Pharaoh seemed to offer a concession of sorts: "Pharaoh responded, 'I will let you go and sacrifice to the Lord your God in the wilderness, but don't go very far'" (Exodus 8:28). In other words, he was telling them to do whatever they were needing to do, but to keep their options open. That way, if they remained close by, they could always return quickly if things didn't work out quite like they had planned. Never negotiate with God to keep your options open regarding whether to follow Him or not; to turn from Him is to return to bondage.

The third compromise of Pharaoh was for the men to go, but to leave their families behind in Egypt. Pharaoh was suspicious of the Israelites and offered for only the men to make the pilgrimage: "He said to them, 'May Yahweh be with you if I ever let you and your families go! Look out-you are planning evil. No, only the men may go and worship Yahweh, for that is what you have been asking for...'" (Exodus 10:10-11). You can be sure Pharaoh realized the subtleties of the compromise he was offering—with fathers in the wilderness and children in Egypt and husbands far away and wives still in Egypt, he knew the men could not give their full heart to worship. Their hearts would be divided between honoring the Lord and love for their families. He also insured the men's return by keeping their loved ones with him. This offer was of no good to the Israelites. It was a half-deliverance at best which was ultimately no deliverance at all.

The fourth compromise Pharaoh offered was for the people to go and worship but to leave their flocks and herds behind. This meant they would be without all that they needed to sacrifice and make their worship complete. Again, there was nothing acceptable about this offer as they would not be able to make their sacrifices to God and their very livelihood was tied to their livestock. By leaving the animals in Egypt, Pharaoh was guaranteeing their return. Worse than abandoning their flocks, Pharaoh knew their worship would be a hollow victory for the Israelites, an incomplete and unsubstantial act of worship. Though he offered for them to all go together, he knew under these circumstances they could not fully serve the Lord. The Israelites were seeking true worship with the Lord. They knew for their act of worship to be complete, they needed to offer all that they had and all that they were to the Lord.

Satan is alive and well and actively engaged in making similar compromises to us all—especially those who have committed their lives to ministry. He is clever and deceitful and knows best where our weaknesses lie. His compromises can come in all sorts of doubts and questions and second-guessing. Some will be theological, causing us to distrust the sufficiency of Scripture or to doubt the validity of Christ's substitutionary death on the cross. Some doubts will arise from the issue of Christ's literal bodily resurrection—was it real or symbolic? Many compromises will come our way challenging us to reconsider, or even cross moral and ethical boundaries. Whatever the bait Satan uses, be on your guard and never compromise your convictions. The promise of the crown awaits the faithful; there is no compromise worth risking it.

4

Don't Panic!

If you're in the ministry for any substantial length of time, there will be times when the challenges before you will seem insurmountable! There will be days and nights when you feel you just cannot go on another day. The opposition seems too strong, the anger too fierce; your peace of mind and heart are threatened and feelings of inadequacy will flood your mind. Stepping away from the ministry seems the only sensible solution—for you, your family and your church.

My word for you is "stop!" Stop in the midst of the chaos; step away from the storms that swirl about you, and never panic. The issues will eventually be resolved, the feelings calmed, and the despair will pass. Stay the course.

Deal with what you can in the short-term, always with kindness and firmness. Address issues and questions one at a time, making progress where you can, accepting where you can't. Find comfort in knowing there is light at the end of the tunnel, no matter how long the tunnel is!

The death and burial of Jesus seemed to herald the end of His ministry, but that couldn't be farther from the truth. His strongest supporters, His disciples, scattered in fear as He faced the cross. All hope seemed to be lost on the Friday night of the crucifixion. But Sunday morning brought with it the hope and glory of the resurrection and the proof that Jesus had conquered death for all. The men who had hidden in fear for their lives emerged and were met with an encounter with the risen Lord. From that moment on, they spent their remaining days proclaiming the truth of the Gospel.

Consider this: It is always too soon to despair. God is always in control. He knows your name, your address, phone number, and email address—including passwords! No matter the battles before you, He has not forgotten you and is still intently working out His plans and purposes for your life. He will see you through it according to His good and perfect will. When you stop to remind yourself of this, you empower yourself to see every cause for panic or despair as an opportunity to draw closer to God. He becomes your strength and stamina, your constant companion. He has promised to never leave nor forsake you!

When you keep by His side, and acknowledge His presence in all areas of your life, His grace will bring consoling peace in the midst of every storm you face. Whatever the storm, don't panic and don't give up. Every storm eventually passes and clear skies always follow.

4

Keep Your Eyes on the Goal

If you don't stay focused on the goal you can easily become distracted by the demands you face every day. Personnel issues, budget concerns, membership problems—all these and more can work their way to the top of your priority list if you don't have an unwavering resolve to do what you were called to do as a minister of the Gospel. In "The Purpose Driven Life," Rick Warren did not mince any words when speaking of our goal—our ultimate goal—as believers: "It's all for Him. The ultimate goal of the universe is to show the glory of God. It is the reason for everything that exists, including you. God made it all for his glory. Without God's glory, there would be nothing." [90]

The great 19th-century Baptist giant John Broadus spoke some immortal words when addressing the almost-certain closure of the Southern Baptist Seminary due to the perils of the country and economy in the 1860s. When he addressed his colleagues about the possibility his words were few, but powerful: "Gentlemen, let us resolve that the Seminary may die, but we will die first." [91] Far beyond his tremendous intellect and international reputation as a homiletical genius, Broadus shared a steely determination and focus that must characterize us all in matters of Christ.

Too many of us are focusing on what's next—the next church, the next position, the next project—that we miss the opportunity of the 'here and now' that is before us. This is not how it should be. Wherever you are, serve every day with the belief that you will spend the rest of your life there. You may not, but you will still have given a lifetime kind of effort to the church and its people. We are to be heirs of this kind of spirit.

From the moment Jesus emerged from His baptism and temptation, He set his face like a flint towards the cross. It was His all-consuming focus, the very reason He came to earth. Despite his repeated efforts and temptations, Satan could not distract Christ from His purpose. And when crowds shouted to proclaim Him a 'bread Messiah,' He didn't for a moment consider abandoning His original mission. Even Peter's efforts to derail Jesus were met with disgust as Christ exclaimed, "... 'Get behind Me, Satan! You are an offense to Me because you're not thinking about God's concerns, but man's'" (Matthew 16:23).

That stinging rebuke reflects more adequately than anything else the intensity of Jesus' commitment to His mission. Jesus loved Peter and had poured much of His life into Peter. Jesus would stay behind after the Resurrection and cook breakfast at the lakeside in order to restore Peter (John 21). Yet the moment Peter tried to intervene between Jesus and His mission, Jesus did not hesitate to make His displeasure known when He used the ultimate insult to call him 'Satan.' Jesus was clear—nothing could or would separate Him from fulfilling His mission.

Charles Spurgeon one said, "The man of one thing, you know is a formidable man; and when one single passion has absorbed the whole of his manhood, something will be sure to come of it. Depend upon that. The desire of his heart will develop into some open demonstration, especially if he talks the matter over before God." [92]

William Mitchell challenged all of us with these words: "Stay focused. Do what you know to do, are called to do, and believe is right to do. Stay focused and persist, no matter what others do." [93]

Never, ever, take your eyes off the goal that God has set before you!

4 Don't Quit

We see reports of war-torn countries around the world and we press on. We can see the increasing impact violence, crime, and drugs are having on our nation, but we press on. We grieve over the immorality that tears at the very fabric of our society, but we will not stop. We are aware of the greed and lust that abounds around us, but we cannot back off. Our nation is preoccupied and addicted to sports and entertainment. We are dominated by politics and deprived of spiritual and theological truth. Our nation and our world is languishing for Christ who is being slowly removed from our consciousness.

The Middle East is exploding as I write these lines. ISIS is rampaging through eastern Syria and Iraq, spreading to Africa and calling for terror attacks against America and its allies. This is a barbaric and violent group devoid of any sense of the value of human life. Their very presence is a danger to every person in their grasp. Yet, we press on! We will not quit! We are in a death struggle with little hope for progress in peace proposals in the Middle East. Russia and the Ukraine remain in turmoil and violence. Iran continues on in its quest to gain complete domination in the Middle East. But we won't be stopped and we won't quit. Keep on! Jesus is Lord and His name must be proclaimed in every place at all times to all who can hear it.

Christ embodied for His followers what it means to be dedicated with an unbending will and an unstoppable resolve to see the Kingdom of God advance. He triumphed in the face of extreme adversity, opposition, and interference. And He asks nothing of us He hasn't also endured. While on earth, His ways were simple as were His needs and wants. He slept mostly outdoors and walked wherever He went. His companions were simple, working-class men, many of whom had been rejected by society. He knew sorrow and grief well.

Jesus practiced His ministry with none of the trappings of modern leaders, not even modern ministry leaders. He lived and died in His humility with the single-mindedness to do the will of His Father by building His kingdom. His commitment to His calling was like Esther's: " ...If I perish,

I perish" (Esther 4:16). He ignored the devil's crowd who offered to believe in Him if only He would come down from the cross. That's because, He knew that God's purpose for His divine redemption could not and would not be complete and accomplished without His sacrifice on the cross.

When face to face with overwhelming and offensive opposition, Jesus refused to quit His calling. With His life on the line and His time literally ticking away, Jesus refused to quit. He stayed the course, suffered the cross, and bought our salvation. If He could endure these unspeakable betrayals, then surely we can face the challenges that come our way without quitting. He is our perfect example. With this as our focus, we can continue.

This verse from Hebrews speaks directly to this:
"Therefore, since we also have such a large cloud of witnesses surrounding us, let us lay aside every weight and the sin that so easily ensnares us. Let us run with endurance the race that lies before us, keeping our eyes on Jesus, the source and perfecter of our faith, who for the joy that lay before Him endured a cross and despised the shame and has sat down at the right hand of God's throne."
–Hebrews 12:1-2

I love the active tense of being faithful Johnny Hunt refers to in "Building Your Spiritual Resume:" "Faithfulness is too often viewed with a past-tense perspective. We look at a person's past and see how faithful they have been; but I want my faithfulness to be active today, and I want my faithfulness to endure until I breathe my last breath…The whole course of our lives should be lived in faithfulness." [94]

Ministry, like much of life, does not take place in the pitch of constant excitement. It is often in the ritual of the routine, in the deadly dull repetition of ministerial duties. Some days, just showing up requires a heroic effort! There are days and weeks and seasons of hard and uneventful work for the cause of Christ. We show up even when we don't want to because of the calling we've received and for the sake of Jesus.

We must ask ourselves, in the middle of changing mores and declining values this question:

Does this kind of flinty aspiration, an unwillingness to surrender, and rock-solid purpose belong only to the heroes of distant generations past?

Or

Will it also characterize us?

Never has the call to depart from our God-given task tempted us more than in this generation. On every hand and from every direction, there are calls for us to abandon our work, taunts that we are fighting a losing battle, and claims our efforts are futile. But still we must fight on. We must lash ourselves to the Word of God and refuse to let the tempting songs of contemporary compromise deflect us from our God-assigned ministry. We cannot quit!

In all likelihood, there will be hours of despair and days of depression. There will be nights of unnoticed and tedious work and weeks of exhausting effort. There will be months of misunderstandings and even years of criticism, but we must not quit.

The devil will tempt us with greed and lust and laziness. He will send discouragements our way and a thousand other temptations, but we must not quit.

We are to be found faithful, no matter what. In doing so, we provide the hope of Christ to the downtrodden and greedy; to the lustful and immoral; to the violent and addicted; and to all who live in our depraved and deprived world. Our hope is their only hope—faith in Christ Jesus. And our call is to stay the course for Christ.

Don't Quit Before You FINISH

Epilogue

Embrace Obscurity

Most of us called to serve in the ministry will not serve in the spotlight of fame and notoriety. We won't have a prominent place in the rankings of ministry positions. Many people will never even know our names or recognize our ministries as significant. Even if all this remains, we must remember that when others do not notice, God always does.

Luke 10 tells the story of Christ's last pilgrimage—his journey to the cross. For this trip, He chose 70 of His followers who were zealous, intense, and enthusiastic for His mission. Once selected, He sent them into Judea to places He would travel on His way to Jerusalem. The thing that differentiates these 70 men from the apostles (besides not being identified by name) is that their assignments were temporary. These men were called to serve, without recognition, over a large territory, for Christ.

Their assignments were different from that of the apostles. The apostles were called to be with Christ, to hear His message, witness His miracles, His sufferings, His death, resurrection, and ascension. They were the ones in the spotlight, the ones we still speak of today. By contrast, the 70 were sent out immediately upon being called to heal the sick and to tell the people the Kingdom of God was near. They were to serve as ambassadors in those places where Christ would soon come.

That's not to say that these men's roles were easy or without dangers. Their roles would involve constant labor, frequent opposition, and oftentimes-intense suffering. This text uses the image of a lamb being sent out among wolves. It is one thing for wolves to come upon a lamb and attack it; it is quite another to be sent into the wolves. The image is one of a defenseless lamb, completely vulnerable, destined for slaughter. Had their journey not been divinely commissioned, it would have been as one walking towards death. However, Christ proclaimed, "Look, I'm sending you…" and because of that they overcame the dangers they encountered.

Most pastors will never serve in a place of prominence where they are known by denominational leaders or as pastor to thousands of members. And for the handful of men who do fill these positions, their prominence is short-lived. As an example, students in a class of about 25 at Southwestern Seminary were recently asked if they knew of W. A. Criswell or Adrian Rogers. Of the students asked, only four had heard of Criswell and five were familiar with Rogers. Dr. Criswell was one of the most well known pastors of the 20th century and Dr. Rogers was one of the leading pastors of the last 35 years, who had only been dead for nine years. Prominent men, among the best known in America, were virtually unknown by upcoming generations.

The lesson is this: Even if we are well known in our generation, we will soon be forgotten! We are not to live our lives for the praise and recognition of others. Our only desire should be to be remembered by God.

The Book of Malachi, Chapter 3, tells of a time when God's people felt alone and abandoned. They gathered together for strength and talked with each other. And then the story goes, "...The Lord took notice and listened..." (Malachi 3:16). What a wonderful promise! The Lord noticed and listened—could we ever ask for anything more? God always observes and listens to His people when they faithfully serve Him. We are never out of God's sight or away from His attention.

Don't allow feelings of insignificance to bring you down. While it is not uncommon to feel overlooked by your community, unappreciated by your congregation, or to even go unnoticed for extraordinary efforts, don't be discouraged. Whether or not the world ever recognizes you and all that you do, God knows you and hears you and surrounds you with His care. God promises to always remember His faithful people; you are never overlooked by Him.

He also remembers His servants perpetually. Just beyond the promise of the Lord noticing and listening in Malachi, it follows that, "...a book of remembrance was written before Him for those who feared Yahweh and had high regard for His name" (Malachi 3:16). The Lord notices, listens to, and always remembers those who honor Him. Above all else, it is the Lord's favor and remembrance we should seek.

The phrase "Book of God" occurs often in the Bible, but only in the Book of Malachi does it mention a "book of remembrance." The Hebrew word is *zikkaron* and it refers to more than just a passive recall by God; it is an active remembrance. When God chooses to remember something, He responds faithfully on behalf of those whom He remembers. God is not only reminded by His book of remembrance, but the very act of remembering causes Him to act faithfully on behalf of His people. God's memory is active as are His actions for His servants.

God also remembers His servants intimately. The verse says the book is "before Him," implying God's remembrance of us is an ongoing process, not a one-time event. He doesn't remember His servants once and never again; He continually remembers them. God's perpetual memory of His people is an intimate memory. When you stop to consider all that is before God—everything in all of creation—it is a mighty thing that the names of His chosen servants remain continually before Him. The universe, the galaxies, the heavenly hosts, Jesus and the Holy Spirit, the entire Church triumphant at rest in heaven, the saints of the ages—all of these are before God. Yet, the names of His chosen and faithful servants are always and forever before Him.

Don't despair if you serve in the shadows of obscurity. It is infinitely better to be known by Christ and remembered by Him than to be known to tens of thousands of men. The memory of man will fade and falter; the memory of God will never dim. But beyond just remembering you, you will also be God's personal treasure as the next few verses tell us:

"'They will be Mine', says the Lord of Hosts, 'a special possession on the day I am preparing. I will have compassion on them as a man has compassion on his son who serves him. So you will again see the difference between the righteous and the wicked, between one who serves God and one who does not serve Him.'"

–Malachi 3:17-18

God not only remembers you perpetually, but He cherishes you as His 'special possession.' The Hebrew word for this is **segullah** and it is used to refer to the king's personal treasure. In ancient empires, the king owned everything and all his subjects were merely tenants. Just by its nature, ownership of everything makes nothing particularly special. If it's all yours, nothing is outstanding.

To guard against this equalizing effect, the king would keep a pouch of valuable jewels in a pocket close to his heart. From time to time, he would take some of the jewels out of the pouch and roll them around in his hand, just to remember that these were, in fact, very valuable stones. The word used to describe these extraordinarily valuable gems is the same one used to represent what we are to him—personal, precious, of indeterminable value. Just as we are this to Him, so also is He to us. When the day is done and the last battle won, the most valuable thing in all of creation to the Lord God Himself will be the special treasure of His faithful servants through the ages.

Success in ministry does not equate to being in the spotlight. Being faithful to whatever and wherever God places you is immeasurably more important. Kent and Barbara Hughes present a similar opinion in their book, "Liberating Ministry from the Success Syndrome." They say, "Scripture consistently links success to obedience—our obedience to God's word." [95]

In speaking to the people in the Book of Malachi, the fact that God saw their ministry, took noticed, and listened, is a great principle for us to remember: most of the faithful servants of the Lord over the centuries have not been well-known by many men at all; they were, more importantly, cherished by God.

- You've probably never heard of Edward Kimball. He was Dwight Moody's Sunday School teacher and eventually led him to Christ. Moody went on to become a world-famous evangelist and founder of the Moody Bible Institute.

- A preaching team from Pacific Garden Mission led Billy Sunday to the Lord. We don't know their names, but Billy Sunday became one of the most celebrated evangelists of the early 20th century.

- Albert McMakin was a farm hand for Billy Graham's father. He convinced Billy to go hear Mordecai Ham preach at a crusade where he was saved.

- Charles Spurgeon was on his way to church when a snowstorm led him to take shelter in a Primitive Methodist Church. An unknown layman preached on Isaiah 45:22 and Spurgeon was saved.

- Evangelist John Hicks preached a revival in far west Texas attended by W. A. Criswell. Criswell was saved there and later became a leading pastor for 60+ years.

- Leonard Dober and David Nitschman were Moravian Bretheren laymen from Denmark and were the first missionaries in the Caribbean. Before they were joined by other missionaries or those who would follow them, 13,000 people were saved and churches begun on most of the islands.

- Charles Finney was well known in the 19th century as an evangelist. He led the best-known revival of the period where some 100,000 souls were saved. He partnered with Daniel Nash for seven years evangelizing. Nash was the front man for the revivals and would often go ahead of Finney and partner with a man named Abel Clary and usually a few others to pray for the coming revival.

Of their greatest revival, Finney said, "The key which unlocked the heavens in this revival was the prayer of Nash, Clary, and other unnamed folk who laid themselves prostrate before God's throne and besought Him for a divine out-pouring." [96]

Despite the thousands that came to belief in Christ, Nash's tombstone is in a neglected cemetery along a dirt road behind an auction barn in upstate New York. No books tell his life story, no pictures or diaries can be found of him or by him, no descendants can be located, and his messages are long-since forgotten, yet his impact on eternity is tremendous! Heaven is considerably richer and fuller for his efforts. Finney left his itinerate ministry within months of Nash's death when he realized the great power of the ministry was lost. Many remember Finney, but few know of Nash.

The great revival in the Hebrides Islands where Duncan Campbell was greatly used of God began in 1949 on the isle of Lewis, the town of Barvas. Two sisters, Peggy and Christina Smith, both in their eighties, couldn't attend the services at their home church because one was blind and the other crippled by arthritis. Instead, they began to pray for a mighty movement of God in their church and on the island. They prayed, claiming Isaiah 44:3.

On the other side of Barvas, seven young men met three nights a week in a barn to also pray for revival, claiming Isaiah 62:6-7. Church pastor James Murray MacKay and church leaders also began praying for God's movement on the island. For months, these three separate groups prayed for revival. The Lord heard their prayers and a great revival swept through the Hebrides Islands from the late 1940s and well into the 1950s. Although many have heard of Duncan Campbell and his role in the revival, most know nothing of the others who prayed so diligently for the island's people.

You've probably never heard of Mike Shillings or Ellis Epps. Both are bi-vocational pastors. Shillings served as pastor of First Baptist Church of Yoakum, Texas, and Epps served in mostly unrecognized positions. However, Shillings was the man who led Ronnie Floyd to the Lord and Epps was the mentor who gave Ronnie many opportunities to preach. Even though Shillings and Epps both served in relatively small environments, their mentorship of Ronnie Floyd was used of God to develop him into one of the most effective leaders in the Southern Baptist Convention.

Returning to the 70 unidentified men Christ called – They returned with joy and reported with much excitement that even the demons became subject to them through the power of the name of Christ. The original word used to convey 'joy' was a much stronger, more emotionally charged word than our modern use of the word. At the time, the word was meant to convey someone who was overcome with joy, filled with joy, or thrilled. It was used to mean a victorious joy—the kind that can only come from the Holy Spirit, not from anything man can provide.

Jesus told the 70 men, "I watched Satan fall from heaven like a lightning flash..." (Luke 10:18). He was telling them this to let them know He observed every moment of their ministry and rejoiced with them in the victories He gave them over Satan. These men did just as they were called and received their due reward: They were willingly sent forth, received Christ's power, and glorified His name; in return, Christ confirmed their report and shared in their joy. As it was for these obedient men, it is for us: There is never a ministry that Christ appoints us to do that He does not carefully observe as we carry it out. He will carefully observe every moment of your ministry because every victory is important to the Lord, no matter how insignificant it may appear to the world.

We will never know who these 70 men were—their names, their lineage, the complete depths of their ministries. Likewise, we'll never know more than just a few of the thousands referred to in the Book of Acts who were scattered when the persecution of the church took place. Though we are familiar with some of the greats in Christian history, they are very few compared to the millions whose names are not known. Like them, you may serve in obscurity, but Jesus sees all ministry done in His name and uses it all for His glory.

These men were given a ministry for a specific purpose and a specific time and place. Throughout their time, they witnessed many miracles. Our commission today places the emphasis on the proclamation of God's saving grace.

The miracles may come, but they are not to be our primary purpose.

Be careful in focusing too much praise and rejoicing on your individual gifts. Too much rejoicing on our gifts, powers, and the effects of our ministry can easily degenerate into pride—possibly the greatest sin in ministry. Pride can become so deadly because it seeks to take credit for what God has given us and what He has done through us. It is an easy trap to fall into and always a danger! The seventy men were always mindful to give credit to the name of Jesus; an honorable example we would all do well to follow.

In the end, the real basis for joy is not the power received or notoriety given in the ministry. Jesus told them, "Don't rejoice that the spirits submit to you, but rejoice that your names are written in heaven" (vs.20). The writer of Hebrews described it this way: "…you have come to Mount Zion, to the city of the living God (the heavenly Jerusalem), to myriads of angels in festive gathering, to the assembly of the firstborn whose names have been written in heaven,…" (Hebrews 12:22-23).

The greatest victories in our ministries are worthless apart from grace. While we understandably rejoice when God blesses our ministry, our first and most personal rejoicing should come from the knowledge that our names are also recorded in heaven. Effectiveness in ministry needs to be held lightly as it is not an eternal joy and subject to the ways and words of man. If you place too much value upon

your personal success in ministry, you must ask yourself
what will happen when things are not going as planned or
disaster strikes. How will you respond when condemnation
and opposition arise?

We all can share in the joy of ministry regardless of
our placement or position. There is room for all in service
to the Lord. Whether gifted and widely known or serving
in obscurity; whether young and energetic or mature and
considerably limited, the ultimate celebration for us all, as
Christ-followers, is the rejoicing that our names are written
down in heaven.

Regardless of where you are in your ministry journey,
ultimately, this is what success in ministry looks like –

- to live in an awareness of His Call;

- to serve Him knowing that He observes every
  moment of your ministry;

- to serve with His anointing and power;

- to serve with clear focus as your name is
  recorded in heaven.

The extent and eternal value of your ministry is not
found in how prominent you are in the eyes of the world. You
may never know, this side of heaven, the extent your service
in obscurity helped to shape others who touched many.

The verses of Ephesians remind us that we, "... were
dead in your trespasses and sins..." (Ephesians 2:1) and that
we are "saved by grace" (Ephesians 2:5). We were lost, but now

we're found. Found and saved, through no merit of our own. Therefore, we have no basis for any pride of accomplishment and owe all to God. Real success is not found in what we do for Him, but in confidence in what He has done for us!

My final words for you, brothers, are this—stay with it! Give it your best. Keep your eyes on the goal and embrace obscurity because God knows you so very well. Whatever else you seek or attempt, remember this—

Don't quit before you finish!

FOOTNOTES

Introduction

1. John P. Kotter, Leading Change (Boston: Harvard Business School Press, 1996), 25.

Section One – You Can't Go if You're Not Sent

2. Elijah P. Brown, Point and Purpose in Preaching (London: H. Revell Company, 1917), 122.

3. Erwin Lutzer, Pastor to Pastor (Grand Rapids: Kregel Publications, 1998), 9.

4. Lutzer, 9.

5. J. H. Jowett, The Preacher His Life and Work (New York: Harper & Brothers, 1923), 12-13, 21.

6. Lutzer, 12.

7. Rick Warren, Purpose Driven Life (Grand Rapids: Zondervan, 2002), 17.

8. Jeff D. Ray, The Highest Office (New York: Fleming H. Revell, 1923), 83.

9. Charles Spurgeon, Lectures to My Students (Grand Rapids: Zondervan 1954), 22.

10. Charles Spurgeon, An All-Around Ministry (Ichthus Publications: 2014), 48.

11. Ray, 68.

12. Charles G. Finney, Memoirs of Rev. Charles G. Finney, (New York: A. S. Barnes & Co., 1876), 25-26.

13. Arnold A. Dallimore, George Whitfield, The Life and Times of the Great 18th Century Revival, Volume 1 (Westchester: Cornerstone Books, 1979), 86.

14. Dallimore, 87.

15. Ray, 82.

16. Rex M. Horne, Jr., ed., Insights from Kingdom Builders (Immanuel Baptist Church, 1999).

17. Horne, Jr., ed., Insights from Kingdom Builders

18. Junior Hill, They Call Him Junior (Self-published, 2005), 81, 84.

19. Hill, 84.

20. Vance Pitman, email to author, June, 2015.

21. Kent & Barbara Hughes, Liberating Ministry from the Success Syndrome (Wheaton: Crossway Books, 1987), 128.

22. H. Harvey, The Pastor: His Qualifications and Duties, (Philadelphia: American Baptist Publication Society, 1879), 164.

23. Michael Catt, The Power of Persistence, (Nashville: B&H Publishers, 2009), 1.

24. J. Kent Edwards, Deep Preaching, (Nashville: B&H Academic, 2009), 43.

25. William Mitchell, Winning in the Land of Giants, (Nashville: Thomas Nelson Publishers, 1996), 115-116.

26. Charles Swindoll, Growing Wise in Family Life, (Portland: Multnomah Press, 1988), 41.

27. James Merritt, Friends, Foes and Fools, (Nashville: B&H Publishers, 1997), 12.

28. James Emery White, Serious Times: Making Your Life Matter in an Urgent Day, (Downers Grove: InterVarsity Press, 2004), 133-134.

29. Warrens W. Wiersbe, Real Worship, (Nashville: Oliver Nelson, 1986), 160.

30. David Putnam, Breaking the Discipleship Code, (Nashville: B&H Publishing Group, 2008), 71.

31. Charles F. Stanley, Living the Extraordinary Life, (Nashville, Thomas Nelson, 2005), 85.

32. Jeff D. Ray, Expository Preaching, (Grand Rapids: Zondervan Publishing House, 1912), 71.

33. John A. Broadus, A Treatise on the Preparation and Delivery of Sermons, (New York: A. C. Armstrong, 1890), 39.

34. S. Parkes Cadman, Ambassadors of God, (The MacMillan Company, 1924), 250.

35. Fred R. Lybrand, Preaching on Your Feet, (Nashville: B&H Academic, 2008), 27.

36. Cadman, 203-204.

37. Arthur S. Hoyt, The Work of Preaching, (London: Fleming H. Revell Company, 1917), 18-19.

38. W. W. Melton, The Making of a Preacher, (Grand Rapids: Zondervan Publishing House, 1953), 32.

39. Hershael W. York & Bert Decker, Preaching with Bold Assurance, (Nashville: B&H Publishers, 2003), 9.

40. Danny Akin, "Integrity in Ministry," Baptist Press News (August 30, 2006).

41. Charles Swindoll, Rise and Shine, (Portland: Multnomah, 1989), 191.

42. George Barna, The Power of Vision, (Ventura: Regal Books, 1992), 72.

43. Warren, 44.

44. Arthur John Gossip, The Hero in Thy Soul, (Edinburgh: T & T Clark, 1928), 7.

45. Adrian Rogers, The Incredible Power of Kingdom Authority (Nashville: B&H Publishers, 2002), 3.

46. Aesop's Fables, The Man, the Boy, and the Donkey, www.taleswithmorals.com (May, 2015).

47. Warren, 29-30.

Section Two – Christian Leadership is Being a Servant

48. Aubrey Malphurs, Being Leaders, (Grand Rapids: Baker Books, 2003), 10.

49. John MacArthur, The Book on Leadership, (Nashville: Nelson Books, 2004), 12.

50. Rogers, 177.

51. Warren, 257.

52. Henry & Richard Blackaby, Spiritual Leadership, (Nashville: B&H Publishers, 2011), 47.

53. Richard Foster, "Celebration of Discipline," Christianity Today, January 7, 1983.

54. MacMillan, 99.

55. Ron Boehme, Leadership in the 21st Century, (Seattle: Frontline Communications, 1989), 59-60.

56. Mitchell, xii.

57. Mitchell, 204.

58. Melton, 73.

59. Kotter, 182.

60. Joseph M. Stowell, Reclaiming a Passion for What Endures: Eternity (Chicago: Moody Press, 1995), 129.

61. Mitchell, 88-89.

62. Christie Craig, email to author, April, 2015.

Section Three – Dealing with Change

63. Gordon Goble, Top 10 Bad Tech Predictions, http://www.digitaltrends.com/features/top-10-bad-tech-predictions/7/ (August 25, 2015).

64. Internet Users By Country 2014, http://www.internetlivestats.com/internet-users-by-country/ (August 25, 2015).

65. Nawsher Khan et al, "Big Data: Survey, Technologies, Opportunities, and Challenges," The Scientific World Journal (July 17, 2014)

66. "Facebook Statistics," http://www.statisticbrain.com/facebook-statistics/ (June 14, 2015).

67. "Statistics," https://www.youtube.com/yt/press/statistics.html (August 25, 2015).

68. Factbrowser.com

69. Factbrowser.com

70. W. Norman Pittenger, The Historic Faith and a Changing World, (New York: Oxford University Press, 1950), 21.

71. Dianna Booher, The Esther Effect, (Nashville: W Publishing/Thomas Nelson Publishers, 2011), 70.

72. David S. Dockery, Christian Leadership Essentials, (Nashville: B&H Academic, 2011), 249.

73. Elton Trueblood, Alternative to Futility, (New York: Harper & Brothers Publishers, 1948), 31.

74. Dr. Richard Land, Racial Reconciliation and the Gospel, http://www.drrichardland.com/press/entry/racial-reconciliation-and-the-gospel (August 25, 2015).

75. J. Wilbur Chapman, The Pastor His Own Evangelist, (New York: Hodder & Stoughton, 1910), 6.

76. Charles Goodell, Heralds of a Passion, (New York: George H. Doran Company, 1921), 55.

77. Charles Spurgeon, Metropolitan Tabernacle Pulpit, Vol. 7, 11.

78. Johnny M. Hunt, Building Your Spiritual Resume, (Woodstock: 3H Publishers), 54.Robert Jeffress, Choose Your Attitudes, Change Your Life, (USA/Canada/England: Victor Books, 1992), 11.

79. Goodell, 16.

80. Alfred E. Garvie, A Guide to Preachers, (London: Hodder and Stoughton, 1912), 186.

81. Melton, 55.

82. Mitchell, 99.

83. Erwin Raphael McManus, Seizing Your Divine Moment, (Nashville: Thomas Nelson Publishers, 2002), 226.

84. Erwin Raphael McManus, Uprising, A Revolution of the Soul, (Nashville: Thomas Nelson Publishers, 2003), 139.

Section Four – This is God's Ministry

85. MacArthur, 113.

86. Barna, 29.

87. Kotter, 68-69.

88. McMillan, 157.

89. Warren, 53.

90. John A. Broadus, The Reformed Reader, http://www.reformedreader.org/rbb/broadus/biography.htm (August 25, 2015).

91. Charles Spurgeon, Spurgeon on Prayer & Spiritual Warfare (6 in 1 Anthology), (New Kensington, PA: Whitaker House, 1998).

92. Mitchell, 128.

93. Hunt, 144-45.

EPILOGUE

94. Hughes, 37.

95. Liardon Roberts, God's Generals: The Revivalists, (New Kensington: Whitaker House, 2008).

Bibliography

Akin, Danny. *"Integrity in Ministry."* Baptist Press News, August 30, 2006.

Allen, David L. *Preach the Word* . Carrollton, GA: Free Church Press, 2013.

Barna, George. *The Power of Vision*. Ventura: Regal Books, 1992.

Barna, George. *Leaders on Leadership*. Ventura: Regal Books, 1997.

Blackaby, Henry & Richard. *Spiritual Leadership*. Nashville: B & H Publishers, 2011.

Boehme, Ron. *Leadership for the 21st Century*. Seattle: Frontline Communications, 1989.

Booher, Diana. *The Esther Effect*. Nashville: W Publishing, a unit of Thomas Nelson Publishers, 2001.

Broadus, John A. *A Treatise on the Preparation and Delivery of Sermons*. New York: A.C. Armstrong & Son, 1890.

Brown, Elijah P. *Point and Purpose in Preaching*. London: Fleming H. Revell Company, 1917.

Cadman, S. Parkes, *Ambassadors of God*. New York: The MacMillan Company, 1924.

Catt, Michael. *The Power of Persistence*. Nashville: B & H Publishers, 2009.

Chapman, J. Wilbur. *The Pastor: His Own Evangelist*. New York: Hodder & Stoughton, 1910.

Dallimore, Arnold A. *George Whitfield, The Life and Times of the Great 18th Century Revival.* Westchester, IL: Cornerstone Books, 1979.

Dockery, David S. *Christian Leadership Essentials.* Nashville: B & H Academic, 2011.

Edwards, J. Kent. *Deep Preaching.* Nashville: B & H Academic, 2009.

Finney, Charles G. *Memoirs of Rev. Charles G. Finney.* New York: A. S. Barnes & Co., 1876.

Foster, Richard. "Celebration of Discipline. Christianity Today, January 7, 1983.

Garvie, Alfred. *A Guide to Preachers.* London: Hodder and Stoughton, 1912.

Goodell, Charles, L. *Heralds of a Passion.* New York: George H. Doran Company, 1921.

Gossip, Arthur John. *The Hero in Thy Soul.* Edinburgh:T. & T. Clark, 1928.

Harvey, H. *The Pastor: His Qualifications and Duties.* Philadelphia: American Baptist Publication Society, 1879.

Hill, Junior. *They Call Him Junior.* 2005.

Horne, Rex M., Jr. *Insights from Kingdom Builders.* Immanuel Baptist Church, 1999.

Hoyt, Arthur S. *The Work of Preaching.* New York: Hodder & Stoughton, 1905.

Hughes, Kent and Barbara. *Liberating Ministry from the Success Syndrome.* Wheaton: Crossway Books, 1987.

Hunt, Johnny M. *Building Your Spiritual Resume*. Woodstock, GA: 3H Publishers.

Jeffress, Robert. *"Choose Your Attitudes Change Your Life.* USA/Canada/England: Victor Books, 1992.

Jowett, J. H. *The High Calling*. London: Andrew Melrose, 1910.

Kotter, John P. *Leading Change*. Boston: Harvard Business School Press, 1996.

Land, Richard. "Racial Reconciliation and the Gospel", Dec. 16, 2014.

Lutzer, Erwin. *Pastor to Pastor*. Grand Rapids: Kregel Publications, 1998.

Lybrand, Fred R. *Preaching on your Feet*. Nashville: B & H Academic, 2008.

MacArthur, John. *The Book on Leadership*. Nashville: Nelson Books, 2004.

MacMillan, Pat. *The Performance Factor*. Nashville: B & H Publishers, 2001.

Malphurs, Aubrey. *Being Leaders*. Grand Rapids: Baker Books, 2003.

McManus, Erwin Raphael. *Seizing Your Divine Moment*. Nashville: Thomas Nelson Publishers, 2002.

McManus, Erwin Raphael. *Uprising, A Revolution of the Soul*. Nashville:

Thomas Nelson Publishers, 2003.

Melton, W. W. *The Making of a Preacher*. Grand Rapids: Zondervan Publishing House, 1953.

Merritt, James. *Friends, Foes, and Fools.* Nashville: B & H Publishers, 1997.

Mitchell, William. *Winning in the Land of Giants.* Nashville: Thomas Nelson Publishers, 1996.

Pittenger, W. Norman. *The Historic Faith and a Changing World.* New York: Oxford University Press, 1950.

Putnam, David. *Breaking the Discipleship Code.* Nashville: B & H Publishing Group, 2008.

Ray, Jeff D. *Expository Preaching.* Grand Rapids: Zondervan Publishing House, 1912.

Ray, Jeff D. *The Highest Office.* New York: Fleming H. Revell, 1923.

Roberts, Liardon. *God's Generals: The Revivalists.* New Kensington: Whitaker House, 2008.

Rogers, Adrian. *The Incredible Power of Kingdom Authority*. Nashville: B & H Publishers, 2002.

Spurgeon, Charles. *Lectures to My Students.* Grand Rapids: Zondervan, 1954.

Spurgeon, Charles. *An All-Around Ministry.* Edinburgh: Banner of Truth Publishers, 1960.

Spurgeon, Charles. *Spurgeon on Prayer & Spiritual Warfare (6 in 1 Anthology).* New Kensington: Whitaker House, 1998.

Stanley, Charles F. *Living the Extraordinary Life.* Nashville: Nelson Books, 2005.

Stowell, Joseph M. *Reclaiming a Passion for What Endures: Eternity.* Chicago: Moody Press, 1995.

Swindoll, Charles R. *Rise and Shine*. Portland: Multnomah, 1989.

Swindoll, Charles R. *Growing Wise in Family Life*. Portland: Multnomah, 1988.

Trueblood, Elton. *The Alternative to Futility*. New York: Harper and Brothers Publishers, 1948.

Warren, Rick. *The Purpose Driven Life*. Grand Rapids: Zondervan, 2002.

Wemp, Sumner. *The Guide to Practical Pastoring*. Nashville: Thomas Nelson Publishers, 1982.

White, James Emery. *Serious Times: Making Your Life Matter in an Urgent Day*. Downers Grove: InterVarsity Press, 2004.

Wiersbe, Warren W. *Real Worship: It Will Transform Your Life*. Nashville: Thomas Nelson, 1986.

York, Hershael W. & Bert Decker. *Preaching with Bold Assurance*. Nashville: B & H Publishers, 2003.

JIMMY DRAPER

Don't Quit Before You Finish